Housecat

How to Keep Your Indoor Cat
Sane and Sound

Housecat

How to Keep Your Indoor Cat Sane and Sound

by Christine Church

Howell Book House

New York

Howell Book House
A Simon & Schuster Macmillan Company
1633 Broadway
New York, NY 10019-6785

Macmillan Publishing books may be purchased for business or sales promotional use. For information please write: Special Markets Department, Macmillan Publishing USA, 1633 Broadway, New York, NY 10019.

Library of Congress Cataloging-in-Publication

Church, Christine.
  Housecat : how to keep your indoor cat sane and sound / by Christine Church.
    p. cm.
  Includes index.
  ISBN 0-87605-142-5
  1. Cats. I. Title.
  SF447.C5 1998
  636.8—dc21   97-46170
                                                                   CIP

Manufactured in the United States of America

10 9 8 7 6 5 4 3 2 1

Book design by A&D Howell Design

Cover design by Nick Anderson

All photos by the author, except where noted.

DEDICATION

For the dog who always loved his cats
Major Bosco's Dillinger, CGC, WAC
10 September 1984–16 October 1997

Though I have had to say good-bye, in my heart you forever remain, no matter where I go or what I do. The cats feel your absence as well. Pounce wonders where his play buddy has gone. We all miss you, my friend, my companion, my love. Be at peace.

A very special thank-you to Carole Rose Werkhoven, DVM, for all her help and understanding.

ACKNOWLEDGMENTS

For my grandmother, whose love of cats was passed to me. Her memory shall live on in my reverence for all animals. And for my mom and dad, who also had a hand in passing to me the love and respect of living creatures.

Thanks to the following for their help with this book:

Veterinarians Dr. Allan Levinthal and Dr. Mostoller

Carol E. Kuehl, Photographer (Candids by Carol) C & G Photo

Sandra Larson, President of Kitty Angels Humane Society
P.O. Box 476
Tolland, CT 06084
(Donations always needed and welcome!)

And everyone who offered tips and/or their personal wisdom.
A special thanks to my editor Beth Adelman for all her wonderful help and understanding.

TABLE OF CONTENTS

PREFACE

Loved and worshipped, hated and feared, cats have been companions to humanity for thousands of years.

A carnivorous mammal in the *Felidae* family, the cat's evolutionary origin is not a clear picture. The most ancient known ancestor is an animal called Miacis, which had a slender body and short legs. As for our own, dear *felis domesticus,* fossils resembling the modern domestic cat, a cross between *Felis sylvestris* and *Felis lybica,* date back some 10 to 12 million years.

The earliest known companion cat dates to about 4,500 years ago, when a cat was buried with its master in an Egyptian tomb. Called *mau,* resembling the sound cats make (the word also means "to see"), cats in Egypt were often mummified and placed in sacred tombs as members of the family. Sometimes mummified mice were placed in the tombs with the cats to ensure their sustenance in the afterlife. In 1890, at one ancient tomb complex in Egypt, 300,000 cat mummies were discovered.

Cats were considered sacred to the Egyptians, who were grateful to them for ridding the granaries of mice. They showed their appreciation by deifying their feline helpers in the persona of a half cat, half woman goddess named Bast.

By the beginning of the Middle Ages in Europe, cats were still tolerated as mouse-catching aids, but by the middle of the 13th century things began to change. Many beliefs and practices of the old pagan religions still existed at the time, and they came under intense persecution. Because the rites of the pagan goddess of fertility, Freya, include a role for the cat, cats too were falsely accused and persecuted. The animals were seen as carriers of evil, brought about by their mysteriously cryptic nature. Witches also came to be associated with cats. This belief led to authorized persecution of cats, and by the year 1400 cats were close to extinction.

This attitude nearly led to the extinction of people, as well, as ships bringing the Crusaders home also brought rats carrying the plague to Europe. The Black Death spread across the continent, and two thirds of the population was exterminated because there were not enough cats left to rid the towns of the deadly rodents.

Cat populations revived after the plague, but cats did not regain the respect and admiration once accorded them by the Egyptians until the mid-1800s, when scientists were able to conclusively prove that bacteria and germs cause illness, not evil spirits or witches. Cats were once again seen in their true light as the epitome of cleanliness.

By the 17th century cats had arrived in America, brought on ships as rat catchers. They were quickly put to work in the New World earning their keep on farms, and eventually found their way back into the hearts of most—loved and honored once more.

Today, there are more than 55 million cat owners in the United States, making cats the number-one household pet. Like the Egyptians before them, many people who own cats treat them with the same respect as any other loved member of the family. Their place of honor and affection in society seems secure.

INTRODUCTION

Growing up in a New England suburb, I always owned cats that were allowed outdoors. The first cat I ever had was in residence with my parents from the day I was born. She was a longhaired orange and white cat named Muffet, and she was hit by a car and killed when I was four years old. I still remember her and the day I stood weeping while my father buried her. Shortly thereafter, we obtained an adorable longhaired tortie and white kitten from a friend's litter. We named her Demie, and she was with me until I was 18. During that time I owned other cats as well, all allowed outdoors.

After Demie passed on, the only cat I had was a male outdoor cat named Bobby who was rarely ever around. He lived mostly outdoors and preferred it there. I wanted a kitten, so I went to the local pet store where I bought Taffy, a shorthaired orange and white female. She was my first experience with an indoor-only cat. I had never even thought cats could be happy living an exclusively indoor existence, but my mother suggested we keep Taffy indoors to prevent any "accidents," as the neighborhood had become increasingly populated. After Bobby was killed by a car, I never again let my cats out unsupervised.

Since then, I have continued to learn, through my cats and others, many new reasons for a cat to live indoors. And I know of an increasing number of people who are also becoming aware of the dangers posed to outdoor cats.

I now have eight indoor cats, all of which are content to live out their lives in the security and comfort of home. As with humans, cats come in many varieties, with many different types of personalities. Some personality traits seem to be inborn in certain cats, and others stem from a cat's experiences. My all-gray male cat, Shadow (affectionately dubbed "Gray Ghost" by my brother), is a shy cat who loves other cats but is afraid of humans. I am the only human he trusts. I have no idea why, since he was born at a no-kill cat shelter and came to me as a foster kitten when he was six weeks old. His entire life has been spent living with utter love and devotion. His brother Sammy, also owned by me, is the opposite in personality. Raised in the same way as Shadow, Sammy is outgoing and personable. Neither of these cats has ever seen the outdoors (except through the bars of a cat carrier door on their annual trip to the veterinarian), and neither has ever shown any desire to step foot outside their safe haven.

Cats who have spent much or all of their life indoors, however, may think they want to explore the outside world (a cat's natural curiosity), but they usually become frightened when actually faced with it. My cat Taffy, though an indoor cat her whole life, always had a fascination and curiosity for the opposite side of the door. This fascination led her to escape unnoticed one day many years ago. I, along with a posse of friends I'd gathered, searched frantically for her, to no avail. I was distraught and worried as to where she could have gone, and my mind constantly relayed unwanted images of what could have happened to her. She was, after all, an indoor cat and unaccustomed to life outdoors. I could not sleep at night and, in my insomnia, frequently ventured into the kitchen to stare out the window.

At 2:30 a.m. on the second day of Taffy's disappearance, I looked out the window and there she was—at the door waiting to be let in, as if she did this every day. I brought her in, where she was warmly welcomed by family members, and afterward I settled into bed with her under the covers, snuggled up against my body. I will never know what she did, where she went or what her experiences were during the two days she was gone, but she never attempted another escape. Apparently, being outdoors was not what she had expected, and she decided the comforts of home were far more delightful than the wilds of the great outdoors.

Most cats raised indoors show little desire, aside from a slight curiosity, to experience what is on the opposite side of that door, particularly if a cat is trained from the start that the door to outside is off-limits to her and a no-no.

At one time it was unheard of to even so much as mention keeping a cat strictly indoors. People mumbled that it was cruel or inhumane to keep an animal with such a wild nature "locked away." Fortunately, this outlook, though still in existence, is waning in popularity. According to a 1996 national survey by the American Pet Products Manufacturers Association, two thirds of all cat owners keep their cats indoors all the time. The number of cats kept exclusively indoors has grown throughout the years, and as the population rises and lifestyles become faster, this number should continue to rise. The survey states that the number of cats kept indoors during the day rose from 58 percent in 1992 to 68 percent in 1996, and the number of cats kept indoors at night rose from 66 percent in 1992 to 79 percent in 1996.

Of course, nothing is perfect, and with the greater popularity of indoor cats comes a whole new set of problems unknown to owners of outdoor cats. But with a little work and lots of love, these problems are controllable and can be overcome.

The key to keeping an indoor cat happy and healthy is the ability to bring to them a world that appeases their natural desires, such as scratching, hunting, sleeping, playing and hiding. This book will discuss the cat's needs and instincts, how they pertain to your cat and what you can do to create the best of all indoor worlds, so your pet can have a productive, healthful and happy life safe from the dangers of the outdoors.

C H A P T E R   O N E

The Indoor Cat: Truth or Myth

Just recently, in a local department store checkout line, the woman at the cash register eyed the cat jewelry I wore on my coat as I placed my items on the counter. "Interesting pin," she said, referring to my gold pin depicting a cat gazing lovingly into a toilet bowl.

"Thank you," I said, and she proceeded to tell me about her two cats.

"They can be such a pain," she continued. "Always wanting in and out of the house."

I offered a simple solution to this problem. "I don't let my cats outside."

At that, she lifted an eyebrow in shock. "I could never do that to my cats!"

"I could never *not* do that for my cats," I offered, before gathering my purchases and leaving.

In its various forms, I have had this conversation countless times. As popular as the concept of keeping cats inside has become, many people still believe that keeping a cat inside is ludicrous, even cruel. This belief

Any cat can live well indoors.

leads to the notion that the quality of a cat's life is diminished if the cat is not allowed to roam free, leading to the assumption that an indoor cat does not lead a quality life. But the truth is that if a cat is raised in a proper indoor environment, it can very well enjoy both quality and quantity of life.

A comfortable indoor environment can be created for just about any cat. There is nothing the outdoors has to offer a cat that cannot be satisfactorily simulated indoors. Sunshine can be brought in through windows, window boxes and outdoor enclosures (see Chapter Seven). Cats can be just as happy chasing catnip mice and interactive cat toys as they can real mice and birds (and they cannot contract parasites and diseases from toys). Cat trees are just as satisfying to a cat as real trees, and cats don't need the kind of room to run that a dog does. Being short-distance sprinters by nature, cats get plenty of exercise running from room to room.

The notion that an indoor cat is "locked up," as if the animal were kept in a prison, is completely false. The cat does not see it this way, particularly a cat that has been raised indoors its entire life. The belief that an indoor cat "suffers" likens the complexity of a cat's mind to the complexity of a human's—and it's not an accurate comparison. To someone watching their indoor cat looking outside at the birds and squirrels,

*For cats, looking out the window
is just like watching TV.*

tail flicking, eyes wide, it may appear the cat is frustrated that she is not allowed out. But to the cat, the window is like a television screen where it can sit and watch a fascinating "movie."

Cats spend three quarters of their life asleep, and often owners of outdoor cats confuse the contentment of an indoor cat's slumber with boredom. Because they do not see their outdoor cat's activities as often, they do not realize their outdoor cat is most likely curled up under a tree somewhere, taking the same catnap she would if she were indoors.

The cat is no longer a wild animal. Humans domesticated cats thousands of years ago. Despite their seemingly aloof nature and independence, cats need humans to protect them from dangers. Most of these dangers were created by humans, and now that cats live with us in our world, it's our responsibility to see to their safety.

Outdoor Dangers

A cat's ability to reason and protect itself in the outdoors is not much more complex than that of a two- or three-year-old child's. They know enough to be fearful of certain circumstances, but do not always know where to look or what to do.

Indoors Only, Please

Shelter workers and those individuals who handle and work with stray, abandoned and ill cats know firsthand the dangers that are posed to an outdoor cat. Some breeders and shelters allow their cats to leave their facility only under the strict condition the cat remains indoors. Kitty Angels Humane Society in Tolland, Connecticut, for example, requires adopters to sign a legal contract stating the cat will remain exclusively indoors (or will be allowed out *only* on a secure leash or in a safe outdoor enclosure).

Of course there are indoor dangers that may befall cats, but those are, for the most part, controllable. As soon as your cat walks out that door, she is no longer under your supervision and is exposed to any danger that may await. The choice, ultimately, is up to the owner, but consider these dangers that are faced only by cats allowed outdoors.

CARS

The number one cause of death and injury to cats allowed outside is cars. Think of everyone you know whose cats are allowed free access to the outdoors and, chances are, at least one of them will have had the horrifying experience of losing a cat, or at the least having their cat injured, by a car. If all those people had not allowed their cats to roam, they would have been spared that particular agony.

Cars pose many threats to cats. Other than just being hit by them, cats seeking a warm, private spot to curl up and go to sleep may crawl into the engine, where they can be maimed or killed if the car is started.

There is another potential danger when a cat likes to curl up and sleep inside the car. Midnight, an outdoor cat from birth, is extremely fond of the comforts found inside a car. She has been inadvertently taken on many trips by climbing into an open car window and curling up in the back seat. One time she disappeared after taking an unplanned trip to work with her owner. Midnight had curled up in the back of his pickup truck, and he drove off unaware that she was there. When he arrived at work, the cat jumped out and disappeared into the woods behind the building. Fortunately, she was recovered four days later.

That trip could have proved fatal to Midnight, as the street her owner works on is very busy during the day. Now all cars that pull into his driveway in the summer are checked thoroughly before being allowed to leave.

DISEASES

There are many diseases cats can contract from other cats or wild animals (see Chapter Eight), most of which may prove fatal to your cat. Some of these include rabies, toxoplasmosis, feline infectious peritonitis (FIP), feline leukemia virus (FeLV), feline immunodeficiency virus (FIV) and feline t-lymphocytic virus (FTLV or Feline AIDS). Some of these diseases, such as rabies and toxoplasmosis, may also be passed from your cat to you. Although preventive vaccinations are available for rabies and FeLV, they are not always a 100-percent guarantee that your cat will not contract these illnesses. And for other illnesses there are no vaccines.

PARASITES

Parasites may be a problem to any cat, indoors or out, but free-roaming cats have a much higher risk of picking up fleas, ticks, worms, lice or mites than cats that are kept indoors. Parasites may also be contracted by your cat if she eats a rodent or wild animal, which is less likely if your cat is kept strictly indoors.

In addition to the damage parasites do all by themselves, they carry many serious diseases. For example, any cat having access to wooded areas may also pick up ticks infected with Lyme disease, particularly in the northeastern region of the United States. Lyme disease may cause serious health complications (for your cat as well as for you) if not caught and treated early.

OTHER ANIMALS

Cats allowed outdoors are subject to wild animals, venomous snakes, insects, dogs and other cats that may fight with, maim or kill your cat. A friend of mine once had her cat come home with his side torn open after an encounter with a neighbor's dog. The cat survived, but not until after much pain, aggravation and costly medical bills.

HUMANS

Humans can be another source of danger for cats allowed to roam free. As much as we love our cats, there are people who don't share the same feelings, and cats allowed outdoors are subject to dangerously cruel pranks or to be stolen for sale to research labs.

Cats might also get into a neighbor's garbage, which could be dangerous to the cat if she swallows bones or a poisonous substance. It will most likely cause bad relations with your neighbors if your cat howls at night, tears at their garbage, walks on their cars with dirty paws, sprays urine on vegetation or digs in their garden. There have been many lawsuits brought against people whose cats have destroyed property and livestock. Even in the country, cats are at tremendous risk when allowed outside.

POISONS

Cats allowed outdoors can crawl under cars and may get oil, gasoline or antifreeze on their coats. As they clean their coats, the toxins enter their bloodstream. Antifreeze is particularly dangerous to your cat, as it has a sweet taste and cats may lick it from a driveway and be poisoned.

Pesticides or chemical treatments on lawns and gardens can also poison your cat, should she walk on a treated lawn and lick her paws.

HUNTING AND TRAPPING

Bajor is a beautiful shorthaired black and white feral cat that now lives his life in comfort at Kitty Angels Humane Society in Tolland, Connecticut. But this was not always the case. Caught in a leg-hold trap before being found and brought to the shelter, Bajor now hops around on three legs.

Areas with hunting and trapping seasons are dangerous to free-roaming cats, as they can't see where a trap may be set any better than a wild animal can. Many cats have been killed or have lost limbs after being caught in leg-hold traps. A cat may also be mistaken for a game animal and shot.

GETTING LOST

As keen as cats' senses and abilities to find their way are, they may still get lost, particularly if you have just moved to a new area or if the weather is bad and the cat gets disoriented (see Chapter Nine for what to do if

your cat gets lost). Unlike dogs, lost cats are not usually recovered. In areas where there are no leash or licensing laws for cats, free-roaming cats are not often picked up by shelter wardens and taken back to the shelter, where their owners can easily find them. And people who see unfamiliar cats roaming may not be as quick to take them in and search for their owners, simply assuming they are "outdoor" cats.

OVERPOPULATION

The overpopulation of cats is a major concern. Millions of cats a year are being euthanized because there just are not enough homes in which to place them all. If your cat is unaltered (not spayed or neutered) and is allowed to run free, chances are good that you're adding to the numbers. Even if you find a "good home" for all your female cat's kittens, you really can't be sure those kittens are not going to produce more kittens that will end up in a shelter or in the street—unless you know for a fact that they are all altered and remain with their families for their entire lives. I've heard people say, "I did my part and found good homes; it's not my problem." Actually, it is. It's everyone's problem. The cats or kittens euthanized in a shelter or starving on the street could have been spared if everyone's pet cats were altered.

Unaltered cats, male or female, are at a much higher risk of injury and danger, as they tend to roam farther and more frequently than altered cats.

It is just as important to have your male cat altered as it is your female. Males are extremely aggressive in their search for a mate and will continue to add to the overpopulation problem throughout their entire lives.

Even indoor-only cats should be altered, as they may get out accidentally. In addition, a female in heat will drive you crazy with her caterwauling and attempts to get out to find a mate. A male cat may spray a foul-smelling urine all over your house, and this odor is almost impossible to remove, particularly from carpets and upholstery.

WEATHER AND NATURAL DISASTERS

In late 1993, Southern California was struck with severe fires that ravaged neighborhoods and destroyed thousands of homes. In some cases, people were evacuated so quickly they had little time to pack or think of what to take with them. Many cats were lost, killed, maimed and injured, particularly outdoor cats whose owners could not find them when it was time to leave.

In severe weather, cats tend to hide and to become disoriented or lost. If a natural disaster such as a hurricane, flood, tornado, earthquake, fire or mud slide should strike your area, it is much more difficult to find a free-roaming cat in the event of evacuation or finding shelter. An outdoor cat may disappear and later return home to find no one there, or worse, no home there. They may get hurt or lost in their attempt to find food, shelter, water or their owners (see Chapter Eight for what to do in the event of an emergency).

Even a cat hiding from a severe thunderstorm can get hurt, disoriented or lost.

SICKNESS

If your cat develops a medical problem, symptoms are much easier to spot if your cat is at home all the time. A cat that is outdoors most or all of the time is usually not around you as much as a cat that lives strictly indoors, so symptoms of illness may not be as evident or as quickly noticed. This can prevent the illness from being caught in time and, with certain sicknesses, early diagnosis is essential to successful treatment.

More Points to Ponder

In addition to the specific dangers lurking outdoors, there are other factors to consider when you weigh the merits of an indoor life for your cat.

LONGER LIFE SPAN

Statistics show that the average life span of an outdoor cat is three to five years, while the average life span of a cat kept indoors all the time is between 12 and 16 years. Considering all the dangers I just mentioned, it's no wonder.

Even if an outdoor cat manages to escape falling victim to one or more of these tragedies, life for the average outdoor cat, even that of a pampered pet, is much more stressful than the indoor-only lifestyle. Cats on the street, or even in the country, are faced every day with territorial disputes and threats from other animals, cats and even people. Outdoors, cats must learn to sleep with one eye open, so to speak, to protect themselves from dangers that may creep up on them in their

The average indoor cat lives 12 to 16
years, while the average outdoor
cat lives just three to five years.
(C&G Photo)

slumber. Indoor cats, however, are usually the epitome of relaxation. I've seen indoor cats fall off fish tanks, television sets and other elevated locations simply because they were so relaxed that their bodies were limp. It's a state of bliss we can all envy!

BETTER PETS

Indoor cats generally make much better pets than cats allowed outdoors whenever they wish. Since indoor cats are with you most or all of the time when you are home, you can both appreciate each other's company a lot more. Cats can be wonderful animals to observe, and what better place to observe their playful leaps and chases than in the comfort of home? Also, because they do not have the added distraction of wanting to go out all the time, indoor cats turn their attention to loving their owners instead of the neighborhood.

A domestic cat is a companion animal, and she should be allowed to be just that—a companion.

Healthy Coats

It's only when I pet an outdoor cat that I realize just how much cleaner and softer my indoor cats are. Not only do indoor cats have less incidence of parasites, but, unless they develop an illness or allergy, their coats are healthier overall, as well. Indoor cats rarely get into anything that soils their coats. They're not exposed to the smog and pollution that outdoor cats are exposed to, either, and it usually shows in their coats with a healthy, luxurious sheen.

Environmental Issues

Many people enjoy watching wildlife, and particularly, birds. They embellish their lawns with bird feeders and baths so as to watch these winged wonders in all their glorious beauty. These people may not appreciate the natural instincts a cat has to chase and kill birds, thus hindering bird-watching for the whole neighborhood. As author Cleveland Amory said in his book *The Cat Who Came for Christmas*, "I feel that no cat owner has the right to jeopardize the right of his neighbor who may enjoy his birds just as the cat owner enjoys his cat."

Roaming cats may also kill endangered species of birds and wildlife. While our pets are descended from predators, cats are domestic animals, and Mother Nature does not limit their numbers in a natural way as She does with wild species. It is up to us, as the ones who domesticated cats, to make sure our pets do not upset Mother Nature's delicate balance by allowing our cats to roam and kill.

LEGAL ISSUES

In some areas leash laws exist not only for dogs, but for cats as well. These laws vary from community to community, and the term "leash law" means different things, depending on the law. For example, some ordinances state that a cat must be confined to the owner's premises, and others state that cats must be kept leashed or caged when out of the house.

Bowling Green, Ohio, developed a cat confinement law in 1984. According to this law, cats should be confined to the owner's property or under the owner's physical control at all times. Also, cats that are leash trained are not to be walked on a leash longer than 10 feet.

These laws are created as a service not only to the cat and cat owner but as a courtesy to the public. Free-roaming cats are not only exposed to plenty of dangers themselves, but also can be an annoyance to neighbors, destroy property and trespass in areas where they are not wanted or can become injured.

Rabies is another issue that has recently been addressed by many laws. In areas with a high incidence of rabies, laws requiring that all cats have vaccines are common. In Connecticut if a cat is picked up outdoors and the owner cannot furnish proof that the cat has been vaccinated for rabies, a fine is imposed.

Making the Decision

Many cats that have spent a good deal of their time outdoors, such as strays and barn cats, may seem as if they simply cannot adjust to life indoors. They can become lonely, bored and destructive. For someone who is unaccustomed to training a cat to stay indoors or someone who is gone most of the time, this task may seem nearly impossible. These owners may become frustrated and feel that although the cat's life may be shortened, the cat will be happier in the long run being allowed outside. However, with patience and proper strategy, almost any cat, no matter how accustomed to the outdoor life, can be acclimated to a life indoors (see Chapter Two).

Of course there are exceptions to every rule, and at times, no matter what the owner does, the cat just insists on having things her own way. I have known of such cats—but very few—and feel, in many of the cases, that the owners did not try hard enough and gave up too soon.

The most effective way of providing your cat with an appropriately appealing indoor environment is to know what your cat, and all cats, would enjoy in an outdoor setting. Cats, by instinct, have certain needs and desires, such as scratching, marking territorial boundaries, eating grass, chasing prey and playing. By providing your cat with the proper equipment, toys, space, attention and love (all of which will be discussed in this book), your cat will have at her disposal a complete environment—indoors.

The decision whether to keep your cat indoors is yours. But remember that owning a cat is a privilege that should not be taken lightly. A cat is not a toy; she is a living animal with feelings and needs. All cats, even ones that spend time outdoors, need and enjoy affection and playtime with their owners. They benefit from interaction, and it will benefit you, as well. Cats are wonderful stress reducers, and that's been proven scientifically.

And as you read on in this book, you will have a better perspective of what it will take to keep your indoor cat happy and make your feline friend the ultimate companion. And you will discover that an indoor cat, if given the proper environment, can truly be a happy cat.

C H A P T E R   T W O

Introducing Your Cat to Indoor Life

Many factors play a role in introducing a cat to life indoors, including the cat's age, personality and how long she was allowed outdoors, if at all. Every cat is a unique individual. The cat's situation will determine the methods and success of converting or acclimating her to a peaceful indoor existence.

Before Bringing Your New Cat Home

Remember how it feels to tear open a birthday gift to find out what's inside? That same excitement awaits the person who is ready to bring home a new cat or kitten. Regardless of whether she is your first or 30th cat, the anticipation is still there. But it is important to remember, for your new cat's sake as well as your own, that certain provisions should be made before your kitten's or cat's arrival. For people already blessed with one or more cats at home, this should be simple, as almost everything needed should already be on hand. But there are still preparations to be made, and the following should always be ready for your new pet:

- Litter pan, litter and liners (see Chapter Four for the scoop on litter and pans).
- Food and water dishes (see Chapter Ten for more information on your indoor cat's nutritional needs).
- Scratching post or tree (see Chapter Five for advice on choosing the best one).
- Cat carrier (for safe trips to the vet or groomer); the carrier you choose should be of a sturdy plastic, rather than the cardboard type, as some cats hate the confinement of a carrier so much they will actually try their hardest to break out of it (see "Carrier Training" later in this chapter for how to acclimate your cat to riding in a carrier).
- Grooming tools (see Chapter Six for grooming and bathing tips).
- Toys (if you're not convinced that toys are vital to a cat's emotional health, see Chapter Three).

Always bring any new cat or kitten to the veterinarian for a checkup and to be tested for feline leukemia virus and feline infectious peritonitis *before* bringing her into your home, especially if you have other cats. Make an appointment to stop by the vet's office right after picking up your new cat.

Cat-Proofing

Although your indoor cat will not be faced with cars, wild animals, cruel pranks or any of the other dangers of the outdoors, houses can hold many hidden dangers, especially to a young kitten that is rambunctious and full of mischief. Kittens seem to have the remarkable ability to find trouble in the most inconspicuous locations.

But unlike outdoor dangers, most household dangers are controllable, and cat-proofing your house before you bring your new cat home can help prevent accidents.

Look around your house carefully and remove anything that may spell danger to your new pet. Use common sense and imagination; try to *think like a cat* when determining what trouble your new cat can get into as you move from room to room. Get down on your hands and knees and look around. Then re-member that cats can jump and climb to high places, too.

THE KITCHEN

The best place to start is the kitchen. Chemicals, household cleaners, detergents, paint, dye, antifreeze, mothballs, bleach, rat poisons and in-secticides may all be harmful to a curious kitty. Kittens, in particular, love to eat the inedible, so anything of potential harm should be kept in an unbreakable container and secured tightly in a closet or cupboard.

Anything small enough to fit into a kitten's mouth (such as milk jug rings or twist ties) should be kept out of your pet's reach at all times.

The stove can be quite hazardous if cooking food is left unattended with a rambunctious cat or kitten around. After cooking, wait until the burners have cooled before allowing your cat access to the kitchen.

The refrigerator is another potential hazard area that should be watched closely. Cats soon learn that food is kept in that big box, and some love to climb inside and see what they can nibble on. As a kitten, Shadow (my curious but shy gray male) took unending delight in climb-ing into the refrigerator every time it was opened. Fortunately, he was always spotted and removed before the door was closed, but such has not always been the case with other cats. Cats have frozen or suffocated to death when trapped inside refrigerators inadvertently closed on them. Kittens are particularly curious and may easily climb inside, searching for the source of that wonderful odor their sensitive nose has detected.

Sharp objects such as knives should be put away and never left out unattended. After washing the kitchen floor, wait until it is dry before allowing your cat to walk on it. The chemicals, many of them poison-ous, can stick to a cat's paws, only to be licked off at bath time. This can make a cat quite sick . . . or worse.

PLANTS

Despite the fact that they are carnivores, cats need to eat some greens. In the wild cats chew on grass to help aid in their digestion, but in the house the only greens that usually are available are your house plants. Providing your cat with her own indoor garden consisting of kitty greens and catnip (preplanted pots can often be purchased from pet supply stores) will help your cat avoid your more treasured plants. But even with these ready-made kitty salad bowls, many cats still prefer to munch on your favorite fern, which is bad for the cat as well as the plant. For this reason, plants should be removed or kept well out of reach, particularly poisonous plants. You may also wish to spray a bitter, non-toxic substance on the plants as a deterrent. Pet supply stores and your veterinarian can recommend sprays made especially for use on plants.

Enclosing the plants behind glass or screens can also help to keep your cat from them. It's a good idea, however, to find out in advance if your plants are toxic to cats. The following table lists some common household plants that are toxic to cats. There are many others, so check to be sure.

Common Toxic Plants

Arrowhead vine	Holly
Boston ivy	Ivy
Caladium	Jasmine
Christmas berries	Laurel
Chrysanthemum	Marijuana
Creeping Charlie	Mistletoe
Creeping fig	Nutmeg
Daffodil	Philodendron
Dieffenbachia	Poppy
English ivy	Spider mum

CHEMICALS

Keep all chemicals out of your cat's reach at all times. Most indoor cats never come into contact with antifreeze, as it is usually kept outside in a shed or the garage. But it's important to know that antifreeze is particularly dangerous because it contains the toxic chemical ethylene glycol and has a sweet taste cats enjoy. That's why antifreeze is best kept where it belongs—outside. Propylene glycol–based antifreeze is a bit more expensive, but it's less toxic to pets.

All spilled chemicals should be cleaned up immediately and the cleaning rags disposed of properly—in bins with tight-fitting lids.

Aerosol sprays should never be used around the cat or around the cat's eating area.

If your house requires fumigation, the cats would be best kept at a friend's or in a kennel for the day until it is safe for them to return. After

fumigating, all eating surfaces and dishes should
be cleaned out and washed with non-toxic detergent; the litter boxes should be cleaned;
and any areas the cats frequent should be
cleaned as well.

If you have your carpets cleaned, keep
your cat off them until they are safely dried.

THE BATHROOM

The bathroom is another room in your house filled with dangers, especially for a small kitten. Deodorants, perfumes, tub and toilet cleaners
and curling irons should be kept out of your cat's reach at all times.

Cats love to drink from toilets, maybe because the fresh, cold water is
always being renewed. Some cats will come running at the sound of the
toilet flushing, anxious for a taste of fresh water. But caution should be
taken with toilets. First of all, toilet bowl cleaner inserts, if used, should
be kept out of your cat's reach; the lid should be kept down on the toilet;
and your cat should not be allowed to drink from the bowl.

Small kittens have been known to fall into toilet bowls and drown, so
even if you do not use toilet bowl chemicals, the lid should be kept down
in households with kittens. Your best bet is to be sure kitty always has
fresh, clean, cold water available at all times in her own bowl, rather
than the toilet bowl.

Human medicines should always be kept away from cats. A cat's
metabolism is much different from ours, and medicines that may help
us can kill a cat. For example, aspirin, as harmless as it may seem to
humans, can be fatal to cats. Ibuprofen is also deadly.

WINDOWS AND BALCONIES

Some cats take delight not only in sitting in windows, but in trying to get
out of them. Windows throughout your house should have secure screens
with a strong mesh so your cat cannot tear them or push them out.

City dwellers beware! Because of a cat's natural grace and tendency
to land on her feet, many people who live in upper-floor apartments
think their cats will not jump or will know to stay away from heights.
But this is not always the case. Maybe the cats see the ground as being
closer than it is or maybe they fall asleep in the window and roll out, but
hundreds of cats every year are killed or injured by falls out of windows.

This phenomenon is so common that it even has a name: high-rise syndrome. Not only do you want to be sure your cat can't get outside, but you want to secure the screens so that they cannot be pushed out. *Never* leave a window open without a screen.

Balconies should also be cat-proofed. Wire-mesh covering on the balcony rails can prevent a cat from slipping off or jumping through the rails.

OTHER AREAS

A cat's legs and body are built for leaping, running and jumping, and cats enjoy viewing their territory from atop high places. Thus, an energetic kitten or cat may spell potential trouble for anything glass, ceramic or crystal in your house. In an attempt to pounce on that unsuspecting bug or imaginary mouse, a kitten or cat may run and jump onto table tops, knocking down anything in her path. My cats sometimes even manage to get on top of the curio cabinet in the living room via the top of the television.

Your home is your cat's playhouse and, as the owner of an indoor cat, you must safeguard your valuables. Even if you train your cat not to jump up onto certain areas, there will still be a time, particularly with a new pet that has not yet learned the rules, that your cat will find these areas irresistible. Keep breakables in closed curio cabinets and hutches and, as I have learned the hard way, don't place anything valuable on top of them.

Fireplaces and kerosene heaters should be covered with safety screens. It is in your cat's best interest to err on the side of caution and make sure the cat cannot come into contact with or be exposed to hot embers or sparks. Wood-burning stoves usually pose little danger to cats, but some cats will sleep so close to a wood-burning stove that their fur becomes hot to the touch.

The paint in older homes can be dangerous, as the lead in paint used many years ago can poison a cat that may eat it. If the paint is chipping and you have the means, repainting should be done before your cat comes home.

Just as electrical cords can be dangerous, so can outlets. Some cats love to chew and explore what to them is an interesting object. Electrical cords hanging within reach are just too tempting. If you have a cat that likes to chew, keep your electrical cords bound tightly and wrapped in

Holidays

During the holidays, extra precautions must be taken to ensure your cat's safety. Any breakable, toxic or harmful ornaments, plants or knickknacks should be kept from the cat's reach or not used at all. Stringed popcorn or beads, as well as the string and needles to make these garlands, can be a threat to your cat's safety.

A rambunctious kitten or cat should be kept away from any decorations or Christmas tree when you're not at home to supervise. And, as mentioned before, be careful with electrical cords and lights.

Holidays can be a hazardous time for your kitty.

aluminum foil or some other material unattractive to cats. Cords can also be run above doors, secured to the wall along baseboards or in some other way fastened out of your pet's reach. (Do not, however, place cords beneath furniture or carpets, or stick tacks or staples into the cord, because this can be dangerous for you.)

Pet supply stores and veterinarians also sell sprays with a bitter taste that can be sprayed on cords, but make sure these are safe to use on

*Always check your dryer before shutting
the door or turning it on.*

the wires before you buy them. In countries such as the United States where outlets do not have on-off safety switches, electrical outlets that are not in use should be kept covered if your cat is particularly curious. Child-proof outlet covers are available at most hardware and department stores.

The clothes dryer can be another hazard for a cat. It's warm and cozy, and many cats will curl up unseen inside. Always check your clothes dryer before putting clothes in and turning it on, and even before shutting the door.

Carrier Training

More than likely, your new cat will be coming home in a carrier. Depending on where you acquire your cat, the carrier may come with the animal, or you may need to buy one in advance. Either way, the chances are good that your cat will not like being confined in a carrier unless she was trained to accept one.

Kittens are easiest to acclimate to carriers simply because kittens are impressionable and the attitudes they learn early on generally remain with them for life. Cats can learn to accept a ride in a carrier so long as they have not already learned to fear and hate carriers.

Generally, the only association cats have with their carriers is a trip to the vet—fear and shots. Negative association. The object behind teaching a cat not to hate the carrier as much as she hates the vet is to teach her a positive association *before* she must be carted off to the veterinarian. To do this, you must introduce your cat or kitten to a carrier slowly and accompany it with positive reinforcement.

There are many kinds of carriers on the market, but airline-approved plastic carriers with wire doors have proven to be among the best types of carriers available.

Although cats don't like to be confined, they do like to sleep in small, confining spaces. If given the opportunity, some cats will even sleep in their carriers. Try simply leaving the carrier open, with a soft towel inside, in a location where the cat is likely to want to curl up and sleep. You can also try playing with your cat in or near her carrier. Place catnip toys inside and even food treats.

Don't expect your cat to accept her carrier in one day. This should be an ongoing process, and it could take weeks, perhaps months, depending on the cat, for her to go willingly into a carrier.

Once your cat seems calm around the carrier, try closing the door and then opening it again. Do this regularly, every day, closing the door for longer and longer periods until the cat can remain calmly in the carrier for 10 minutes or so. Next, lift the carrier with the cat in it, and carry it around the house a bit. Once your cat is comfortable with this process, try taking the carrier, cat inside and door firmly locked, outside for a small walk around the yard. All the while, speak to the cat and reassure her that this is fun and no harm will come to her.

Eventually, you can move the process up a step to taking the cat into the car. Set the carrier on the front seat and start the engine. Have toys and treats ready to distract your cat should she seem nervous. Don't open the carrier; place the treats through the bars in the door, or use a feather toy waved in front of the door for the cat to watch and bat at.

Next, take a little trip with the cat. Just a short trip at first, five or 10 minutes. Make the trips longer and longer; maybe one trip per week. Don't overdo it.

Even though your cat now accepts the carrier and maybe even goes willingly into it, don't limit trips only to the vet, or the cat will eventually figure out that is what the carrier is for and will learn to fear it. Since most cats will only need about one trip to the vet a year, that gives plenty of time to take your cat for the occasional fun trip. Don't forget the treats and toys, even on trips to the vet.

Bringing Kitty Home

At first, your cat may be apprehensive about being in a new place. This is normal. If your new pet is a kitten, then most likely she has not been away from momma long. If your cat's an adult, she's likely to be more wary of change than a kitten. Depending on the cat's personality and past, she may either run and hide, crouch low to the ground and explore, or take immediate charge of the household. In any case, leave the cat alone for awhile in the beginning to let her grow accustomed to your home at her own pace.

I'll look first at how to introduce your cat to a household with no other pets. Then I'll discuss what you can do to welcome your cat into a multi-cat household.

SHY CATS

Maybe you acquired your cat as a stray, or maybe the cat is feral or came from an abusive situation before you adopted her. If this is the case, your new cat may be more shy and apprehensive about this new place she has been brought into. Although almost all cats may be shy in the first few days, a cat from one of these situations may take longer to adjust and will need more love and reassurance than an outgoing cat.

More than likely, a shy cat will hide when you first bring her home. Leave the cat alone for awhile and go about your business. Don't have any parties or large gatherings of people in your home for awhile, as this may frighten the cat more. She will need time to learn that you are trustworthy.

Your new cat will likely choose a hiding place where she feels safe—maybe inside a closet, under a desk or behind a bed. If the cat won't come out of the haven she has chosen after a day has passed, place her food, water and litter box near the spot she has chosen (make sure this place is safe and comfortable; if not, move the cat to a more convenient location). This will give the cat more reassurance that she doesn't have to expose herself to the open in order to take care of her needs. When you can, sit with the cat, pet her and speak in a soothing tone (but do not allow a crowd to gather around, and never allow children to run around near the cat).

Don't give up hope. When your cat is ready, she will come out and explore. This may take anywhere from a day or two to weeks, maybe months, depending on the cat. When I first brought home my cat Precious, she was so shy she stayed hidden whenever anyone was in the house. She would only come out to eat or use the litter box at night or when no one was home. It took six months before she was trusting enough to mingle with the rest of the family. After that, she would only hide when company came. Now, years and lots of love later, she trusts and loves everyone in the house and even visits with most strangers.

Eventually your cat's natural curiosity and instincts will bring her out of her shell. Not all cats will learn to trust strangers, but with the proper introductions, time and patience, they will love you.

APPREHENSIVE CATS

Some cats will be curious yet apprehensive about entering a new home. These cats will generally crouch low to the ground as they explore their new environment, seeming to contradict their own movements. As with very shy cats, leave the cat alone at first and don't have any company or parties until the cat is comfortable. You don't want to frighten an apprehensive cat into becoming a shy cat.

After a few hours, show your new pet where her food, water and litter box will be kept. You may have to show these items to the cat several times in the next few days, particularly with a new kitten, but cats are quick learners. It will be easier if you have other cats in the house, as they will lead the newcomer to where these essentials are located.

OUTGOING CATS

Some cats will need practically no introduction. These are the outgoing types that will enter your home and take

Apprehensive cats will crouch low to the ground as they explore. (Beth Adelman)

over almost immediately. These cats seem to learn more quickly where their litter box is, and particularly where that delicious food is kept. It is not that they are more intelligent than a shy or apprehensive cat, they are simply more extroverted and have no qualms about going for what they want.

However, even if your new cat seems immediately at home in her new surroundings, she will still need guidance and adjustment time for those first few precious days. It is still wise not to allow parties or excessive noise, and always show a new cat or kitten where her litter box, food and water will be kept.

Introducing People

After your cat has become accustomed to, and accepted, her new home, it will be time to introduce other family members, pets and house rules. But remember, always allow your new pet time to adjust. This period of adjustment will vary with each cat. As mentioned before, shy and apprehensive cats should be left alone, except for love and reassurance from you, until they're ready to wander out on their own. When you feel your cat is ready, introduce people and other pets slowly, if possible.

FAMILY MEMBERS AND CHILDREN

The procedure for introductions will again depend on the individual cat's personality. For shy cats it is best to introduce adults first, one at a time. If the adult has already been spending time with the cat while she is in hiding, then introductions may not be necessary. If not, or if the person is a stranger to your home, the adult should always sit on the floor before an introduction is made. This position is less threatening to the cat and brings the person more to the cat's level. The adult should stroke the cat gently and speak soothingly until the cat is comfortable. With some cats this may take several tries. Never force the cat to stay if she does not want to. This will only frighten a shy animal more. Also, make no sudden moves or loud noises around the cat.

This type of introduction also works with apprehensive and outgoing cats but should not take as long to accomplish, so long as nothing frightens the animal. Always be gentle with any introductions, no matter what the cat's personality.

I recommend that you do not acquire an extremely shy cat if you have young children, as they are naturally rambunctious and cannot understand how important it is to be calm and quiet around such a cat. Children will be excited about the new addition to the family and will want to play. This seemingly harmless activity may have serious consequences for a shy and withdrawn cat.

However, if a cat of this type has fallen into your care and you have young children, it is very important to supervise all activity in the cat's presence. Hold the child's hand and you can both stroke the cat gently, showing the proper way to pet a cat. Explain that this is a living being with feelings and not a toy. Never let several children gang up at once on any cat, particularly a shy cat. Teach them to pet the cat one at a time and quietly.

Even with outgoing cats, a child should be taught to be gentle and how to handle and stroke the cat. Even a harmless ear or tail tug can result in painful scratches to the child. The difference with an outgoing cat, however, is that she will likely grow accustomed to the noises and activity level of children more easily and quickly than a shy or even an apprehensive cat.

> ### *Taking Care*
>
> A cat should not be acquired solely for the purpose of teaching a child responsibility. If your child forgets to do the dishes, they can pile up for a day or two in the sink. But a neglected cat suffers needlessly. Always supervise to be sure the cat is being fed properly, fresh water is given and the litter box is scooped or changed regularly.

Teach all children the proper way to pick up a cat; by placing one hand under the cat's hind end and the other hand just under and behind the front paws, lifting gently. This should be done with the child sitting down at first, so the child does not drop the cat and can get used to the procedure. And make sure children understand they should not pick up the cat unless it is absolutely necessary, and they certainly should not carry the cat around the house.

Remember, young kittens may scratch or bite when they play. A child should learn how to tell when a kitten (or a cat) has had enough and wants to be left alone.

CATS AND BABIES

I'm still amazed at the number of people who think they must give up their cat because they are expecting a baby. This is partly due to a few myths that still persist about cats and babies. Pregnant women are often told they must give up their cats because of the threat of toxoplasmosis, a disease that can cause birth defects in children. It's true that toxoplasmosis can be spread to pregnant women through the feces of a cat, but it can easily be avoided with care. If you are pregnant, either avoid cleaning the litter box or wear rubber gloves when doing so, and always wash your hands thoroughly afterwards. It's that simple.

Jealousy (on the part of the cat) is another common misconception that can be avoided or lessened. Your cat is part of the family, and some cats may become jealous when a new baby comes into the home (see Chapter Three for more on jealousy). If possible, you should introduce your cat to baby sights, sounds and smells before the baby actually arrives. You can set up a tape recording with the sound of a baby crying, play with your cat around baby toys and maybe create a "mock day with the baby" where you do the kinds of things you'll do after the baby arrives.

Once the baby comes home, don't forget to give your cat plenty of attention. It's probably a good idea to keep the cat out of the baby's room and away from the crib unless you are there to supervise. Cats love to curl up where it's warm, and this could be in the crib with the baby. As much as your cat may be trying to show affection to the new child (cats can and do fall in love with babies), a 10-pound cat lying atop a small infant can smother a child.

The fact that cats love to knead with their paws to show contentment, lay on top of a child's warm body and at times taste the milk that may be left behind on a child's mouth, has been the genesis of many a strange myth (such as the myth that a cat will "suck a baby's breath away"—completely *false*). Once the child is old enough and big enough to handle the cat's weight and to knock the cat off if he or she chooses, then the main caution is to prevent scratches or bites by teaching the child how to behave around a cat.

Meeting Other Cats

Introducing your new kitten or cat to other household pets is a different matter. You cannot explain to your other pets how to behave around the new family member, so introductions must be made carefully. All cats react differently to new arrivals. Some will be accepting, others indifferent, and still others defensive.

My neutered male cat Pounce hisses with the arrival of new adult cats, but loves kittens. I foster many kittens before they are placed in homes, and Pounce takes it upon himself to make them feel right at home while they are here, even allowing them to "nurse" on him while he bathes them—just like a mother cat. Most males are not as maternal as Pounce, but some females may be. I've even known people whose kittens "nurse" on the dog.

If you are obtaining a new kitten or cat as a companion for a resident kitten or cat, try to find one with the same personality, manner and activity level, and near the same age.

Many experts suggest getting a male cat for a female and vice versa. However, once cats are altered (castrated or spayed) it usually does not matter. Many shelters nowadays alter kittens through an early spay/ neuter program, so you will not have to worry about having it done later. Spaying or neutering a young kitten is not dangerous to the animal and is becoming more common as a way to reduce the numbers of unwanted kittens.

It is easier to introduce kittens into a household with other cats than it is to introduce an older cat. Even so, whether you adopt a kitten or a cat, the following method is suggested. This introduction method can take anywhere from a couple of hours to a day, depending on the reaction of the cats to one another.

Place the newcomer in a separate room with food, water and a litter box. If the new cat is in a carrier (which she should be) and is reluctant to come out, allow her to stay there. Leave the door to the carrier open and exit the room.

Cats use scent as a communication tool, "reading" the pheromones secreted from another cat's glands. Letting your resident cat(s) sniff around the door of the room the new cat is in will help the cats to identify one another before meeting face to face. Do not be surprised if, despite the door between them, there is much hissing and spitting among all cats. This is normal and should not cause you much alarm. If a towel or a blanket came with the newcomer (or anything else with the cat's scent on it), set it down for your other cat(s) to inspect.

Feeding resident cats near the base of the door will help them to associate something pleasant with the new cat's scent. Give your resident cats plenty of attention during this time so they will not feel abandoned. Visit the new cat frequently as well for calm reassurance.

When all the cats have relaxed, move your new cat to a different location in the house. Allow resident cats to enter the room your new cat was in, so they may sniff around and become more accustomed to the scent.

Once the cats begin to appear more comfortable with each others' scent, try placing your new cat in a carrier with a barred door and let her and your other cat(s) smell each other through the door. Again, expect plenty of hissing and growling.

The next step is to let your new cat or kitten mingle with resident cats, but keep a close eye on them. Feeding them together might help. Some experts recommend placing butter on the new cat to help persuade resident cats to lick her and learn to accept the new cat. However, never force new cats together.

If you have the room in your house and the time to spend, you may want to try moving your new cat to a different room each day for several days until her scent fills the house before allowing her to mingle face to face with your other cat(s).

If you acquire a kitten and have an older cat, watch them closely. A spunky kitten may pester an older cat relentlessly. When I first brought my cat Pounce into the house as an eight-week-old kitten, he would romp around attacking the older cats even as they were trying to sleep. Some of the cats were very patient with him, others were not. Even as an adult cat, Pounce is rambunctious (some cats don't outgrow kittenhood as quickly as others) and he still tries to play with the older cats, whether they want to or not. Now they are accustomed to his ways, and he usually receives one of two typical responses from them: Either he'll be humored with play, or he'll find a paw swiping across his face followed by a hind-end view of the offended cat walking away.

An indoor cat that is an only cat may be even less patient with the antics of a young kitten than cats in a multi-cat family are. Keeping the kitten busy with toys and games, or acquiring two kittens, might help take the pressure off the older cat. However, in some cases a kitten will actually bring out the frisky in an older cat. Some of my older, more sedentary cats became like kittens again after Pounce came into the house.

A new kitten, like Willie, can make an older cat like Mukti (who is 20!) feel like a kitten again. (Natalie Chapman)

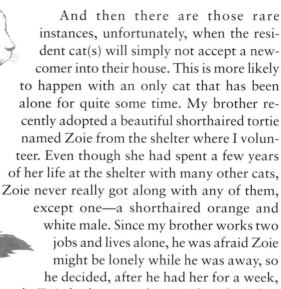

And then there are those rare instances, unfortunately, when the resident cat(s) will simply not accept a newcomer into their house. This is more likely to happen with an only cat that has been alone for quite some time. My brother recently adopted a beautiful shorthaired tortie named Zoie from the shelter where I volunteer. Even though she had spent a few years of her life at the shelter with many other cats, Zoie never really got along with any of them, except one—a shorthaired orange and white male. Since my brother works two jobs and lives alone, he was afraid Zoie might be lonely while he was away, so he decided, after he had her for a week, that he would adopt the male Zoie had gotten along with to keep her company. Apparently Zoie, who had taken over my brother's home from the moment she arrived, did not agree with this idea. The cat she got along with so well at the shelter was suddenly an intruder in "her" home. She hid constantly, hissed whenever the male (whom my brother named Shemp) tried to play with her, and her loving nature turned aggressive.

It was unfair to Shemp for my brother to keep him, as it was obvious after a week that this situation was not going to work. Shemp, being a social, playful cat, could not understand why Zoie wanted nothing to do with him and, with my brother gone most of the time, he grew lonely. Painfully, my brother gave Shemp back to the shelter (where he was later adopted to a wonderful family and receives the love and play he requires), and Zoie took over the house once more. Her loving nature returned and she is again happy.

Some cats simply prefer to be alone. Although Zoie plays with my brother as if he were another cat ("attacking" his arms and pouncing on him), she still prefers being *head cat* in the household. My brother is all she needs, and she is perfectly happy this way. And my brother, who really only wanted one cat anyway, found the perfect roommate.

Give your new cat time to adjust (ideally two to four weeks) and see how things go. If plenty of time has passed and it becomes obvious that one or more of your cats will simply never get along, that the cats are completely miserable in one another's company, you may need to return the new cat (if possible). As painful as this decision is, it's better than allowing the cats to live in misery together.

If returning the cat is not an option and you are determined to find a way to get these two cats to at the least tolerate one another, you may wish to try a cat therapist. Yes, there are therapists for animals and sometimes they can work with you and the cats to come up with a solution. Ask your veterinarian or a shelter professional if they know of any cat therapists in your area.

Other Animals

Introducing new cats to other animals, particularly with dogs, requires more caution than when introducing a cat to another cat. When you bring a new cat into a home that already has other animals, your priority should be the safety and security of all involved. You don't want your dog to injure your cat, but you also don't want the cat injuring your hamster or bird.

Dogs

Some cats and dogs seem to be natural friends, others natural enemies. Pounce, the odd one that he is, absolutely loves my mother's Siberian Husky. Pounce has been seen kneading the dog, burying his face in the dog's fur and rubbing against the dog's face.

But not all cats will take to dogs as Pounce does. If you are introducing your new cat to a dog that has never been around cats before, introductions will require care and patience.

Introduce the cat at the dog's eye level, holding both carefully. If the dog seems agitated or aggressive, remove the cat and try at another time. *Never* leave the cat and dog unsupervised until they are perfectly comfortable and accustomed to one another. Even an overly playful larger dog that is accustomed to cats may inadvertently injure a cat or kitten, so close supervision is essential.

There are, on occasion, times when the dog and cat will not become accustomed to one another, no matter how much time and patience you have. If this is the case, it would be in the cat's best interest to find her a more suitable home.

Usually cats that have grown up with a dog or a puppy are more likely to become friends with another dog. If you acquire a puppy, things

*Dogs and cats can get along fine
when they are raised together.*

should go a bit smoother with introductions. A puppy, like a kitten, has not yet fully developed the instincts he will have as an adult, and the most trouble you will probably run into is the puppy's unending energy. A puppy will see your cat as another puppy to play with. Although a cat is intelligent enough and able to defend herself if the puppy becomes too rowdy, a declawed cat, an ill cat or a more sedentary cat may not be able to defend herself or get away from the puppy's advances. Be careful that the puppy (particularly a large breed) does not harm the cat with his enthusiasm to play, or wear an older cat out with constant demands.

BIRDS, REPTILES AND RODENTS

It is not necessary to actually introduce your new cat to these types of pets unless they will be interacting regularly. Even so, these pets should be kept in secure cages and out of your cat's reach.

As with dogs, use extreme caution when introducing these types of pets to your cat. A cat's natural instincts are to play with or even kill these animals, depending on the cat's background and personality. I have had pet rats and I could allow them to interact with some of my cats, but not all. My cat Precious, who was once a stray, has still retained her hunting instincts. I had doves that I had to find a new home for because, with Precious in the house, I could no longer let them fly free (the other cats had never bothered them). I didn't think it fair to the birds to keep them caged all the time, so I gave them to a friend who had no cats—only other birds for them to fly with.

Some cats will never be able to interact with "prey" animals safely. Others will mother these pets and treat them as if they were the cat's own babies. To introduce a rodent, bird or reptile to your new cat, hold the pet carefully and watch the cat's response. If her instinct seems to be to attack, take the animal away. Otherwise, let them interact and keep a close watch.

Never, never leave a cat unsupervised with a small animal, no matter how good the relationship between them.

FERRETS

Ferrets and cats usually get along great with little introduction. In my experience, however, it's usually the ferret, with its playful and rambunctious nature, who intimidates the cat. Make sure the cat is not frightened of the ferret and the ferret is comfortable around the cat.

Ferrets have extremely tough skin and can play very rough, not understanding that the cat's skin isn't as rugged as their own. Generally, more active cats will get along best with ferrets. My cats Pounce and Shadow are so rambunctious that the ferrets have the same energy level. When I take the ferrets out, those cats are right there wanting to play with them. At times Pounce even gets too rough for the ferrets.

As with any other animal, supervise play activities carefully until the animals are accustomed to one another and you are positive no harm will come to either pet.

Cats and ferrets can be great friends. Just make sure you supervise their interactions.

Setting House Rules

It has been widely stated that cats are incapable of learning house rules. This belief is fueled by their seemingly aloof nature and tendency to want things done their way. It is also not wholly true. Cats are intelligent animals and are quite capable of learning rules and even tricks when taught properly and with patience.

Persistence, patience and consistency are the keys to teaching house rules to cats. It is important to remember that any rule (such as not jumping on counters) you want your kitten to follow in adulthood must be taught right from the start. Try not to give in on the rules just because the kitten is cute or the cat is new to the house, only to punish the cat later when the novelty of owning her has worn off. A cat does not understand why she was allowed on the table or counter as a kitten and is punished for the same behavior as a cat. You'll want your cat to know the rules you've established as soon as possible.

When I turn the lights out at night, I generally am sharing my bed with at least four cats in various locations around me. I love it, but not everyone wants their cat to share their bed. Maybe they have mild allergies and need to keep the cat away from their sleeping area, or maybe they have a particularly rambunctious cat that loves to chase toes in the middle of the night. Whatever the reason, simply keeping the door closed does not always work unless the cat has been well trained from kittenhood to stay out and not try to bang the door down when it is closed.

Cats hate closed doors (unless the door has always been closed to them and they are accustomed to it). Their natural curiosity makes them want to get on the other side, even though they know what is there. But, as with any other rule, teaching the cat to stay out is a task that requires patience and persistence. A cat that has always been allowed in the bed-

room and suddenly isn't anymore will probably not accept this change lightly. She wants to be with you and does not understand why she suddenly can't. She may wail and cry outside the door, scratch and try to stick her paws under the door, as if she can lift the door up enough to slip under. You can try keeping the cat in another room, but chances are her wailing will keep you up anyway. Here is a good example of why you must decide what rules to set forth for your cat *before* you bring her home.

PLAY AND MESSAGES

Often what is viewed as aggression, whether among cats or between a cat and a person, is really cat play or the cat's way of relating a message the only way she knows how. Some cats, if they do not wish to be patted at that moment, will suddenly attack your hand for what seems like no apparent reason.

In play, sometimes a cat will run at you from out of nowhere and "ambush" your leg. If you do not like this behavior, you must work with the cat at as young an age as possible to stop it. A quick squirt of water (if you know when the cat will "attack") or a shake at the scruff of the neck can give your cat the message you are upset. Often stomping your feet or yelling at your cat will halt the behavior quickly, but with some cats this may cause a neurotic behavior or fear of your feet—or you.

CORRECTIONS

When training or correcting a cat, *never* hit or use extreme physical force. A cat will not associate the punishment with the crime, and may grow fearful of you while retaining the behavior you wished to stop. A good correction tool is a water pistol or spray bottle filled with water. Most cats hate being sprayed with water and will quickly learn that getting up on the counter or scratching your sofa will result in a squirt.

But the water trick only works when you catch your cat in the act. Do not correct a cat or kitten for a mistake she made a minute or an hour before. Even if you drag your cat to the scene of the crime, she will have no idea what the correction is for—cats simply don't associate things the way we do.

If, however, your cat learns to stay off the counters only when you are around, you might want to keep her in another room when you are away, at least until she learns the appropriate rules. You can also try placing a substance on the inappropriate area that is unpleasant for the cat to walk on, such as aluminum foil or double-sided tape. Some companies sell pads that give off slight electrical charges. These pads are made to place on surfaces you want to keep your pet off. After several shocks (which are no more than the shock you get from static electricity), your pet will find that surface undesirable, even after the pad is removed.

Cat Beds

If you want your cat to have her own bed, there are many to choose from. Most pet supply stores sell cat beds, and there is usually a vendor at every cat show who sells them as well. Cat beds range from pads you can place anywhere you wish to wicker baskets or elaborately decorated and colored cat "palaces." Whichever bed you choose, it should be soft, comfortable and washable.

Some beds have cedar mattresses to repel fleas. However, they are not recommended, as cedar can cause respiratory problems in some cats.

Keep your cat's bed clean and dry; cats are meticulously clean, and most are opposed to sleeping in soiled areas. This includes cleaning the frame of the bed as well as the pad. You can buy a bed with removable pads that can be thrown in the washing machine, or you can place a towel inside the bed. Some beds are entirely washable.

You cannot make your cat sleep in a particular location, so placing the cat bed where the cat spends most of her sleep time will help make sure the bed is used. Sprinkling catnip on the bed and playing with the cat in it will also help create a pleasant association with the bed.

Most cats prefer your bed to theirs.

Crate Training

Crate training is usually associated with dogs, but kittens can be crate trained as well. An adult cat that has not been in a cage before will most likely not accept a crate and does not need one, so it is best to limit crate training to kittens.

A crate is a cage, either an all-wire cage or a large airline-approved carrier (usually a combination of wire and plastic). The crate should be large enough so the kitten has room to play, and it should also accommodate a small litter pan, food and water dishes and the kitten's bed. The largest size dog crate works best.

Why would you want to crate train your kitten? For times when you are not at home or if you want a good night's sleep, crate training is a good idea. Kittens want to play at all hours and get into mischief frequently. Crate training will give you peace of mind and prevent the kitten from harming herself when you are not there to supervise. Crate training also teaches a kitten to eventually accept cat carriers.

Kittens do not resent being confined and will generally sleep in their crate even when the door is left open. The crate should be lined with a soft towel or blanket, which should be kept clean and dry. Place the crate in a draft-free area away from crowds and traffic in your home.

Acclimate the kitten to her crate by keeping the door open on the first day and showing the kitten where the crate is and that it contains food and water. Place the kitten inside and play with her, speaking softly. Try closing the door, but if the kitten seems to panic, open it again. You do not want any negative associations with the crate, which will eventually become your cat's own special place. You can continue trying the next day.

If the kitten seems reasonably content, walk away for a few minutes, then return a few moments later and open the door. Continue this throughout the day, leaving the kitten for longer and longer periods of time. At night, place kitty in the crate after playtime and when she is tired. Walk away, leaving her alone with her thoughts. Make no fuss, even if she cries, and soon your precious little bundle of fur will be sound asleep. Make sure your kitten has plenty of play time and family interaction outside the crate most of the time.

Never use the crate for punishment or keep the kitten in it for extended periods of time, such as when you go away. Also, if you work full-time, your kitten should not be kept in the crate all night and all day.

Find another way to keep the kitten out of trouble, such as confining her to a large room equipped with toys, food, water and litter pan and with all dangers removed.

As your kitten grows, learns the rules and becomes less rambunctious, allow her more and more time out of the crate until you no longer need it. A full-grown cat usually will not get into the trouble a kitten will and should not be confined. Once your cat no longer uses the crate, you can remove it or leave it open all the time (your cat may prefer to sleep there). I have crate trained three of my adult cats from kittenhood, and all still sleep in any crate or carrier they can get themselves into.

Acclimating to the Indoors

Each cat is unique, as are their circumstances before they came to you. Many times, this previous situation plays a vital role in shaping the cat's personality and will have an effect on how well the cat adapts to indoor life.

Once your cat has become accustomed to your home and settled in as one of the family, you will want to take into account the cat's previous situation, if known, when you decide how best to acclimate her to life as a housecat. Following are some of the most basic situations a cat may have faced, and the best methods of getting your cat accustomed to being indoors all the time. Whether you've acquired a kitten that has never seen the outdoors or an adult cat that has lived outside all her life, with love and patience you can teach your cat to live happily in the safety of home.

KITTEN—NEVER BEEN OUTDOORS

This is the simplest situation to deal with. A kitten adjusts much more readily to new situations than an adult cat, and one that has never been outdoors will not be constantly trying to escape. In this situation, you simply acclimate the new kitten to your home, as described earlier in this chapter.

There are some kittens, however, especially as they reach adolescence and become more curious, that will try to get out when they see you going in and out the door. Their curious nature will make them want to know what is so fascinating that keeps you wandering out there. I had this problem with my cat Taffy for many years, until she got out and discovered life was a lot better indoors. Sometimes a cat outgrows this curiosity, but why wait and risk an escape when you can do something about it now?

One way to deal with this problem, besides giving the cat plenty of toys to keep her occupied and cat trees to climb on, is to make a rule that outside doors are an inappropriate area for the cat. A water squirt bottle is effective here. Stand outside the door and open the door a small crack. When your curious feline comes too close, spray the cat with water, then slam the door. This, combined with a *verbal* reprimand or even slamming the door hard whenever the cat gets near, should help to keep her away. Let your cat know this is one of the rules: Doors are off-limits. But remember, as with any training, be patient and consistent, and *never* hit your cat with anything.

Kitten—Previously Lived Outdoors

Although kittens adjust quite easily to most situations, one that has spent a great deal of time or all of her life outdoors (such as a barn cat, feral or stray cats) may need a period of adjustment to accept her sudden confinement indoors. Even at a young age, cats become accustomed to their environment. Acclimating a strictly outdoor kitten to indoor life will require patience and persistence.

First, you will want to go through all the steps outlined in the previous section ("Kitten—Never Been Outdoors") to acclimate the kitten to your house and to teach her that the door outside is an inappropriate location.

As an adolescent, a young outdoor cat might be more persistent at trying to escape than a young kitten. They know what goes on outdoors and are usually not afraid of what's out there.

Keeping a close eye on all those who come in and out of your house will be crucial in the beginning. Your new kitten or adolescent cat might try the dart-quickly-out-the-door-when-it-opens routine. Let everyone who may come in or out know about your cat. Combine this with plenty of indoor activities such as toys, cat trees to climb, window perches, balls to chase, etc. Once the kitten has grown into adulthood, she will be plenty satisfied with indoor life and will most likely forget about trying to escape.

Sometimes adopting two kittens around the same age will keep their minds off wanting to go out, as they will be too busy playing with each other.

ADULT CAT—NEVER BEEN OUTDOORS

This is the easiest situation for acclimating your new pet. An adult cat that has never been outdoors will not think she's missing anything. The cat will already be accustomed to life indoors and will need very little adjustment. All you need to do in a situation like this is to acclimate your new pet to your house, make sure she knows where the food, water and litter are, and teach her the house rules.

ADULT CAT—ALLOWED OUTDOORS

Sylvia was a stray outdoor cat that lived in the woods behind a yacht club. One day she just strolled down the dock, tail held high, as if she owned the place. We already had 11 cats in our house when Sylvia "found" my mother and stepfather. They took her onto their boat, which was docked at the yacht club the week they were there on summer vacation.

Probably because she had always been an outdoor cat, Sylvia had no idea what to do with the litter box my stepfather placed in the boat for her. Instead, she woke him in the middle of the night so he could take her outside to do her business. When the week was up, and after she had been checked over by the veterinarian who had a practice beside the yacht club, my mother and stepfather brought Sylvia home.

In the beginning we were concerned that she might not accept her sudden confinement indoors. We underestimated her. Sylvia took to indoor life completely, learned immediately (maybe from the other cats) what that "sand box" in the house was for, and never again showed even the slightest desire to go outside.

Often, strays have had enough of the outdoors. That's why they seek out human companionship. They have learned the hard way that the freedom of the outdoor life is not all it's cracked up to be, and they prefer the quiet life of a housecat, as long as their needs are met.

Generally, cats that were once strays accept life indoors fairly readily. It is as if they realize they have been given a second chance and are eager to take it. The real challenge is in acclimating a resident cat that has previously been allowed outdoors to an indoor life.

The Good Life

Precious was an outdoor cat when I found her as a stray. After she finally overcame her fear and got accustomed to the house, there was no way she wanted to explore the outdoors around this new environment. If a door was opened near her, she would run in the other direction. To this day she still does. Of course, cats like Precious and Sylvia need no indoor acclimation. They know a good thing when they find it.

Whether you adopt a previously outdoor cat that still wants out, or you wish to convert your resident outdoor cat to an indoor life, there are some definite steps you will need to take. This is a difficult situation for the cat, which is a creature of habit. Restricting the movements of a cat that was once allowed to roam sometimes breeds what animal behaviorists call *confinement stress* (see Chapter Three for more on cats and stress). Suddenly being forced to stay inside is always quite a shock to a cat like this. The cat may become destructive, cry a lot and try to escape every time a door is opened.

It may seem cruel to some people to try to keep a cat like this in, but it will really depend on you and the cat. You will need much patience and persistence, and a gentle yet firm manner.

For some cats, gradual acclimation to the indoors (bringing them in for longer and longer periods at a time) will work best. For others, being allowed outside even occasionally will only encourage the cat to want to go out more. In this case, it's best to bring the cat in and keep her there. If you live in an area with seasonal changes, the best time to do this is as winter approaches, when the cat will want to be inside more anyway.

Distract the cat away from doors as best you can. Your cat will need an overabundance of love, attention and distractions. Find out by experimentation which toys and games are your cat's favorites, and set up playtimes each day when the cat is at her most active. Try to re-create indoors the things your cat would normally be doing if she were to go outdoors (cat trees, cat grass, toy mice, ramps to run up, etc.). If all of your cat's desires are satisfied indoors, she will eventually find no need to go out and will settle into a quiet routine.

One word of warning here, though. A previously outdoor cat may never stop, at least on occasion, trying to slip outside. If possible, you might want to build an outdoor enclosure (see Chapter Seven) that will at least give your cat safe access to outside and stop her from being interested in slipping out of doors.

SPECIAL SITUATIONS

You may wonder why a previously outdoor cat would need to be brought indoors permanently (other than the very compelling safety reasons), but at times certain situations arise where this is the only practical solution.

A cat that is extremely shy upon adoption, even if previously an outdoor cat, may become frightened in a new situation and, when let outside, could get lost or disoriented.

There are people who are considered accident prone, and cats can be as well. Some cats just seem to find trouble wherever they go. A friend of mine once had a cat that, whenever he went outside, would come back scarred from a cat fight, mauled by a dog or injured by a car. Eventually her only choice was to make him an indoor-only cat. If you have a cat that continually gets into fights with neighboring cats or other animals, it will probably be in the cat's best interest to keep her indoors.

A cat with a contagious or debilitating disease should also be kept in the house full-time. If your cat tests positive for feline leukemia, or is infected with any one of the other contagious diseases that can afflict a cat, she should be kept indoors to prevent infection to other cats. A cat with a debilitating disease, or any illness that may affect her senses or responses (such as epilepsy), should be kept indoors for her own safety.

Handicapped cats should always be kept indoors. A cat with a missing limb cannot run as quickly should danger threaten. Blind or deaf cats do not have the necessary senses for dealing with the many dangers the outdoors has in store.

If you adopt a blind cat (as I did with Teisha) or if an illness or injury blinds your cat, acclimating the cat to your home, or to life indoors, will require a little more effort than with a seeing cat. You might want to show the cat where everything is at first. Give her a space that is all her own—a space that's not too large—until she becomes accustomed to getting around.

When I first acquired Teisha, she took shelter under my bed and was too frightened of the other cats to come out and eat—or even to use the

litter box. I moved her haven to the cubbyhole beneath my computer desk and placed her food, water, bed and litter box there. Slowly, as she adjusted to the house and other cats, she began to come out and wander on her own. I eventually removed the litter box (as she was by this time using the other ones along with the rest of the cats). Then, as she chose new sleeping places, particularly my bed, I removed the towel I had placed under my desk. Now Teisha has the run of the house. She knows where everything is and manages to get around almost as well as the seeing cats. And this is delightful to see. Imagine my amazement when I came into the living room one day to find six cats perched in the bay window, all watching intently the many birds in the feeders outside, and Teisha there in the middle of them—facing in the opposite direction and purring so loudly I could hear her from across the room. I imagine that she thought she was looking at the birds outside with the other cats, when in reality she was staring into the living room. I'll never ruin her fun by telling her the truth.

Remember that your best tool is always patience when teaching any cat to live indoors, no matter what the animal's situation may be. Once both of you have adapted to each other, you can enjoy fun, games and many years of indoor enjoyment together.

The Cat's Mind

Physically, a cat is much healthier when she stays indoors. But what about the cat's emotional health? In certain situations, the stress of confinement can cause behavioral problems and weaken the cat's immune system, making her more susceptible to disease.

Every cat has moments of stress, whether severe or slight, temporary or permanent, that must be overcome. With an indoor cat, the signs of stress are more apparent than in the outdoor cat—particularly if they are displayed in a destructive manner—and you can work with your cat to do something about them.

Stress is a natural part of existence, both human and animal. Cats adjust well to indoor life if they have the proper essentials to fill their needs. But a cat that has lived most or all of her life outdoors and is converted to an indoor cat may show more stress-related behavior than a cat that has never seen the outdoors.

To prevent, reduce or eliminate stress, it helps to know why cats react as they do; what innate behaviors are responsible for their actions, likes and dislikes.

Your cat's development and socialization began with momma. Through contact and observation with first her mother and siblings, then with other cats and even humans, a kitten learns important behaviors that will shape her personality as an adult. This includes not only feeding, hunting, grooming, litter box habits, playing and scratching, but also socialization, fear and aggression. Kittens with little or no human contact in their first four to seven weeks of life often never fully trust humans. Kittens raised only by humans often never develop proper skills of socialization when dealing with other cats. All these factors play a part in a cat's eventual personality and stress tolerance level.

Certain types of aggression (such as mock play between kittens, which prepares them for dealing with other cats later in life), defending territory and scratching are examples of behaviors normal to a cat, yet these can be seen as undesirable to their human owners. When these behaviors become a problem in the household (urinating outside the box or becoming aggressive suddenly, for example), often the underlying cause is a physical problem or stress.

If your cat is showing signs of stress-related behavior, taking the time to find out what and why is the first step in solving the problem. Is your cat stressed because she was only recently converted to an indoor cat? Or is your longtime housecat suddenly showing signs of stress? If so, ask yourself some questions and try to pinpoint the cause. What has changed in your life or your cat's? Has the cat been ill? Have you recently acquired a new pet? A baby? A spouse? New furniture? New cat litter?

Cats are intuitive and pick up on the emotions of others around them. Many times we will unknowingly create stress for our cats because of the stress in our own lives. Cats are proven stress reducers for humans, lowering blood pressure and calming the nerves. But, at times, in our effort to use our cats to alleviate our stress, we actually transfer the stress to them.

What Causes Stress?

Cats are creatures of habit and love their routine. Some cats adjust more readily to changes than others, but even the most aloof and sedate cat will experience some stress when something in her life has changed. Stressful change can be physical, emotional or environmental. To combat any of these stressors, you first must recognize the cause and then treat it appropriately, with patience and perseverance.

Causes of Stress

Physical	Emotional	Environmental
Showing	Jealousy	Moving
Breeding	Death (human or animal)	Crowding
Illness or injury	Separation or divorce	New family member (animal or human)
Parasites	Feline rivalry	Confinement
Surgery	Boredom/loneliness	Loud noise
Obesity	Competition for affection	Lack of fresh air and sunshine

Let's take a closer look at some of the more common stressors that affect a housecat. Later in this chapter, I'll explain how you can help your indoor cat combat problems due to stress.

Feline Rivalry

In an ideal situation, cats in a multi-cat household will play together, groom each other and share mealtimes happily. The more cats that come into a household of indoor cats, however, the higher the incidence of stress and the greater the possibility of feline rivalry and aggression.

Though cats living in a multi-cat household will establish a pecking order, often forming little groups, close proximity can cause tempers to flare and the fur to fly. Even in households with only two or three cats that generally get along, there will be the occasional spat.

In my household some of the cats have formed these little social groups, while others prefer to remain solitary. Cats that are closest in age or were raised together are usually the ones that will get along the best. They form a hierarchy within their own little group and display behaviors that indicate the true nature of the domestic cat as a social animal: mutual grooming, and sleeping and playing together.

Cats are rumored to be solitary creatures, but anyone who lives with multiple cats or who has seen the boredom and behavioral problems of cats that do not receive enough social interaction (human or animal) knows otherwise.

*Cats in the same group can be very social
with one another. (Ellen Cringle)*

Social structures can also shift as time goes by. Cats, as they age, may grow apart and no longer share activities as they once did. My oldest cats, Taffy and Candy, are a good example of this. Raised together as kittens, they once shared everything: sleeping space, food, playtime. Now they barely tolerate one another. They hiss, spit and swat at one another if one gets too close. No specific event or change triggered this, but rather it came about gradually as the cats aged and more cats arrived, shifting the social structure of the household.

Arguments in a cat society where two or more cats share the turf is normal, even necessary, to settle disagreements and establish a hierarchy. As normal as this behavior is, however, stress can still result, particularly when one of the solitary cats is being bullied by a cat from a group. Usually disagreements are settled on their own, with one of the cats walking away with little more than a scratch on the nose.

Feline rivalry, whether a harmless quarrel or an outright fight, can be caused by many factors. Let's take a look at the most common ones.

TERRITORY

Territorial disputes are a common problem in multi-cat households. If a new cat comes into the house, often the social structure will shift, causing a temporary disruption in the hierarchy. Introducing a cat should be done carefully, as outlined in Chapter Two. Simply throwing new cats together is an invitation for trouble. They may eventually work it out, but why start things out on a rough note and cause more stress for your cats?

Any threat to a dominant cat's territory, even from a close companion, can cause disagreements. It's common to see spats over places in bed with you, sleeping rights for the comfy chair, a spot on the couch and so on. Cats generally sort these disagreements out themselves without much problem.

If you feed strays or if strange cats come into your yard, occasionally this will also upset the cats in your house. In this case, one or more of your cats may quarrel with one another, sometimes viciously, or even with you. If you really must feed strays near your home (getting them to a shelter would be a better option), feed them out of sight of your indoor cats.

PERSONALITIES

Misinterpretation of intent causes spats as well. As much as cats enjoy mutual grooming and playing, even this can turn into a disagreement. I have often seen this with my cats. One will be grooming the other, or they will be playing nicely, but one will decide she has had enough. If the other continues, a brief tiff ensues until one gives in and walks away. This type of argument generally flares up and is over quickly, with no harm done to either cat.

Sometimes cats just simply do not get along. Personality clashes are common in multi-cat households, particularly where there are three or more cats. Any change in household routine can upset the balance of the cats' hierarchy and raise stress levels, which may make cats more testy with one another.

Some cats are just bullies. A cat considered lower in the pecking order by another cat may be bullied relentlessly by the stronger, more assertive cat and may even have to be separated, either temporarily or permanently.

COMPETITION

Competition for food is a common cause of feline rivalry in a multi-cat household. Ensuring that each cat has her own food dish will not always solve this. Some cats simply want to eat from their friend's dish and will sometimes even pull the dish away with a swift paw.

Competing for owner attention and possession of toys can also cause the occasional spat; one cat wants what the other has.

SCENT

A cat that has recently been outside, say to the veterinarian, will come home carrying a different scent. This can sometimes temporarily confuse the other cats in the household, which might even think the returning cat is a newcomer. Usually this is only a temporary problem and will resolve itself in a day or two as the home scent once again returns to the cat.

Restoring Peace

So what can you do to solve disputes among your cats? If the problem only occurs at certain times or during certain activities, then a temporary "time out" or separating the cats at that time may help. For instance, if the cats fight over food or one cat steals from another, you may want to separate the more dominant cat just during meals. This can include feeding the cat in a separate area of the kitchen or in another room altogether.

Sometimes it's necessary to simply let the cats work out the differences on their own. If it's just a quick little spat and no one is getting hurt, don't worry. Allow the cats their space and they will solve their differences quickly.

Separate cat trees or trees with multiple levels will help solve disputes over sleeping quarters. Most cats will choose a favorite place to snooze, and providing enough places per cat should ensure the "top cat" stays on top, therefore calming territorial disputes.

If two cats are fighting relentlessly, or one cat bullies another, sometimes a quick squirt with water will separate the fighting cats. But this usually will not stave off any further problems. Some people who have the room to do it separate the fighting cats permanently as an alternative to getting rid of one of the cats. My cat Shadow was fine as a kitten, but as he grew into adulthood he began bullying my oldest female Taffy, to the point where she would rarely come out of hiding. I set up a room for her away from him with her food, water, litter box and sleeping area. I would take her out so that she could sleep

Calming Herbs

Some people have used homeopathic medicines and flower remedies to alter their cat's behavior and calm frightened or belligerent attitudes. Some shelters use these remedies to calm feral cats and newcomers to the shelter.

Bach Flower Essences Rescue Remedy is the original flower remedy (there are imitations) and is available at health food stores or by contacting Bach Flower Remedies, Division of A. Nelson & Co., Ltd., Oxon OX14 5JX, U.K.

Though they should be used only in extreme cases and not permanently if possible, certain antidepressants are also available to calm the nerves of a particularly stressed cat. These should *only* be given under the direct supervision of a veterinarian.

and play in the bay window during the day and sleep with me on my bed at night. Now, a year later, I keep the door open, and she comes and goes as she pleases. Shadow has learned he is not allowed in "Taffy's room," and she feels more secure knowing there is a special place she can go if he begins bullying her.

Overcrowding among cats can cause a lot of arguments and territorial disputes. Moving to a larger house will give you and your cats more room, but this is not always a feasible solution. So if you can help it, don't bring more cats into the house than you can handle or your resident cats can get along with. Most experts recommend one cat per room of the house, but this depends on the size of the house, the size of the rooms, the personalities of the cats in the house and how much you can handle as far as care, feeding, attention and vet bills.

One of the best stress reducers, for both you and your cats, is play. Even cats that live with many other cats benefit from interaction and play with their owners; particularly the cats that may not belong to any social group formed among the cats in your home. Cats respond very positively to love and attention. Take time out, for yourself and your cats, to play with them, pet them and show them your love each and every day.

Loneliness

The opposite of the feline rivalry problem is the only-cat syndrome. When Taffy was a kitten, we also had another cat, Bobby. But Bobby, being an older outdoor cat, was hardly a suitable playmate for a feisty kitten. After several weeks, we started to notice a change in Taffy. She didn't play as often and was beginning to become lethargic. She tried to play with Bobby the few times he came into the house, but he would simply swat her away and she would slink, bereft, downstairs to stare at the wood stove. She was lonely and needed a companion.

A little more than a month after we acquired Taffy, we got Candy. Being close in age and activity level, Taffy and Candy needed no introduction. Young kittens rarely fight even when presented to one another on the spot. After a short acclimation period to the house, Candy was ready and willing to be Taffy's playmate and companion, and Taffy couldn't have been happier. Her activity level picked up, and Candy and Taffy became inseparable.

Some cats, such as my brother's cat Zoie, prefer being the lone cat and will not accept another cat on their turf. But even such independent, solitary cats can get lonely and may begin to exhibit signs of stress. Cats

A cat alone can get lonely. (Beth Adelman)

in multi-cat households, particularly those outside the hierarchy of a group, can also get lonely. Usually these cats prefer human companionship. But if their human is away much of the time, the cat may become stressed and bored.

Behavior for a lonely or bored cat varies from lethargy to destruction. Like Taffy, some cats will simply stop playing and mope around the house. Other cats may become destructive or aggressive.

Often only cats will "attack" their owner in mock play, as if the owner were another cat. This is a cat's way of recognizing the owner as a member of the cat's pack. Since there are no other cats to play with, you are your cat's only source of interactive amusement. For some cats this works out well, and they are perfectly happy with this arrangement.

Often this mock attack-play goes no further than the occasional incident and causes no harm. In itself this may not be a sign the cat is bored or lonely. Shadow, although he has many other cats in his pack that he plays with daily, still enjoys an occasional "battle" with my arm or a swipe at my legs as I walk by. There is no harm in this; he is recognizing me as another cat, which to a cat is quite an honor.

But with a lonely or bored cat this behavior can sometimes get out of hand. The cat may start to attack viciously or become downright nasty. This kind of behavior should not be encouraged, particularly with children in the house. A cute young kitten's innocent scratches can become painful wounds (which may lead to infection) as the cat grows older and bigger.

So, what if you already have an only cat that will not accept another cat or kitten into the household, yet is beginning to show signs of boredom or loneliness? If you can, pay more attention to the cat. I know this sounds obvious, but I am still surprised at the number of people who don't pay enough attention to their cats. Because of the cat's seemingly aloof nature, it seems as if they need no one. But nothing could be further from the truth.

If you are away much of the time (due to a job or something else that cannot be helped), make sure the cat has plenty of toys to play with that will keep her occupied throughout the day, cat trees to climb, greens to nibble and windows to look out. Besides these, you may want to try leaving the TV or radio on when you are away. Soft music has been known to reduce stress and relax cats. There are even videotapes available that you can play for your cat. Some of these show birds, squirrels

Fish tanks can provide a cat with entertainment, or simply a warm place to sleep.

and wildlife scenes, which, the video makers assume, will entertain a cat. Watch your cat's reaction to these tapes, and you'll know if they were right.

Some experts recommend obtaining a different kind of pet for your cat, such as a fish. My cats will sit for hours on top of or beside the fish tanks, staring at and trying to catch the fish. Just make sure the tank has a secure lid, or the fish may become a snack rather than a pet.

Small animals such as hamsters or gerbils won't be much use as a companion for a cat. Although some cats may enjoy watching the tiny animal in its cage, the cat's presence will most likely scare the animal more than benefit the cat. Ferrets, as mentioned in the previous chapter, are sometimes good companions for cats. However, be sure the two get along well, and even then it's not a great idea to leave them alone together when you're not home. Also, check the laws in your area; ferrets are illegal in some states.

Be careful, too, with dogs. Although some cats love dogs as companions (my cat Pounce absolutely adored my Doberman Pinscher and my mother's Siberian Husky) and they will get along great, some dogs will not appreciate a cat as a companion. Usually dogs and cats work out best as companions for one another when they were raised together.

If there is a tree outside your house (or a balcony, if you live in an apartment on a higher floor) you may want to place bird feeders where the cat can watch safely through a window or door as the birds come to visit (in a city this may be pigeons, but the cat doesn't care).

Jealousy

If you have ever seen a sudden change in a cat's behavior when a new person or pet came into the home, you were more than likely witnessing a jealous reaction. Any change to a cat's comfortable position in the home that may take away the owner's attention can cause jealousy. Even a simple change, such as a shift in job hours or scheduling, can upset a cat's normal routine.

I know a woman who got in the habit of playing with her cat every morning before she went to work. One morning she was running late and did not have time for the usual routine. She laid her work clothes out on the bed and went into the bathroom to get ready. When she came back into the bedroom to get dressed, she found the cat had left a "present" waiting for her right smack in the middle of her clothes.

Cats grow accustomed to the love and affection they receive from their owners. Living with a cat has often been likened to raising a child, and for good reason. Cats thrive on love, attention and security as much as a child does. Jealousy is a powerful emotion, and when an event occurs that interferes with a cat's comfortable routine, often insecurity will result and the cat will show her disapproval the only way she knows how. Usually this means inappropriate behavior, such as urinating or defecating outside the litter box, or scratching where the cat knows she is not supposed to scratch (not to be confused with a cat that simply has not yet learned the proper place to scratch). Those are the most common behaviors a jealous cat will exhibit, but other signs can also indicate a cat is unhappy about something. Some cats will go off their food, mope, stop grooming themselves or become destructive.

A new baby in the house is a common cause of jealousy in housecats, especially if the cat is accustomed to regular attention from her owner. A cat does not understand why this tiny wailing person is taking up all her owner's attention. A cat that has a companion she spends much of her time with (preferably another cat) will probably not be as affected by this change as a cat whose owner is her whole world, but even in a two-cat family, more attention from the owner can mean the difference between upset and comfort.

A new spouse or another pet in the house can also upset a cat's world. During a time of change, a cat may feel her security and place in the household are threatened. But you want your cat to be accepting, not put off, by the new addition to your house. Thus, the cat will need even more attention than she usually gets. This attention gives your cat something to take pleasure in as well, and will remind her that nothing has changed in your heart and she has nothing to fear.

Death and Divorce

Cats are extremely sensitive creatures, often sharing in silence the pains of their owner. When something has happened to upset a cat's person, often the cat, too, will feel upset. This puts stress on the cat, and as hard as it may be when you are feeling bad, the cat will require extra attention and love to get through this stressful period. Your cat can benefit you just as well. Remember, the love and attention you lavish on your cat during a difficult time can benefit you, too. The act of petting a cat has been scientifically proven to reduce stress, alleviate depression and lower blood pressure in humans. During low periods you need your cat just as much as your cat needs you, and this is a good time to sit in quiet contemplation with your cat in your lap, relaxing.

Therapy Cats

Although dogs are most commonly used in pet therapy programs, cats are becoming popular for visits to nursing homes and hospitals. The results of these visiting pet therapy programs are staggering. To watch a person who is generally withdrawn and depressed suddenly come out of his or her shell while petting a cat is an emotional experience.

Signs of Stress

Each cat is an individual and will exhibit signs of stress in her own way. Destructive behavior is one symptom I've already mentioned, and there are many others. But there are some general symptoms to look for. It's important to recognize that these are stress behaviors and are not simply your cat acting willful or naughty. Then the trick is to find out why your cat is developing behavioral problems and to address them (the earlier section "What Causes Stress" should help).

Remember, too, that whenever you see a change in your cat's behavior, it is important to first rule out any physical ailment. If the cat receives a clean bill of health from your veterinarian and obvious stressors are not apparent (or are eliminated) but the cat is still exhibiting a change in behavior, then you will have to do a little detective work. Your cat cannot tell you if she is feeling down, but she will show you in other ways.

REFUSING TO USE THE LITTER BOX

This is the most common way cats exhibit their stress. Many times the stress stems from too many cats sharing a litter box, competition from other cats or another cat picking on the affected cat and thus causing her to fear going to the box. Giving this cat her own box may help.

This problem can also stem from a previous physical illness such as a urinary disorder or bowel problem. A cat with a urinary or bowel problem may find it painful to urinate or defecate, and thus associate the pain with using the litter box and begin to avoid it. Even after the illness has been successfully treated, the cat may still be afraid of using the box. If this is the case, carefully retraining the cat may be required.

Other litter box factors that can stress a cat include the brand of litter used, how clean the box is, the location and size of the box, the use of litter liners and the number of boxes per cat. See Chapter Four for complete litter box information.

A recently declawed cat may not want to use the box, as the litter can hurt her sensitive feet. Temporarily replacing the litter with a softer substance (such as sawdust, sand or shredded paper) can help (see Chapter Five for more on the issue of declawing).

If your cat is six months old or older and is not yet altered, you may be seeing signs of a cat's natural tendency to mark territory. Cats are

 territorial, and urination is an innate behavior used for marking boundaries. Cats altered before sexual maturation are less likely to develop this habit.

Senior cats may have more difficulty holding their urine. A vet trip may be in order, as he or she may be able to prescribe a medication to help your cat.

Your veterinarian may also recommend certain tranquilizers or medications to help modify an inappropriate behavior such as indiscriminate urination.

OVERGROOMING

Often, when a cat feels stressed, she will take her frustrations out on herself, either by excessive licking or overgrooming. Some cats will overgroom to the point of making themselves bald, or opening sores on their skin.

LOSS OF COAT CONDITION

A cat's coat is a good indication of her well-being. If a cat is ill or under excessive stress, her coat will shed more heavily and become dull. She may groom excessively or not groom at all. Often a cat's skin will flake and the fur will shed when the cat gets nervous or upset. If you've ever taken a cat to the veterinarian and ended up almost as furry as your cat, you already know about this.

LISTLESSNESS

A normally active cat, when under stress, might become listless and mope around the house, actually acting depressed. Many times a cat will refuse to play—even her favorite games. Listlessness is common in cats that have recently experienced the death of a person or pet close to them, but any one of the stressors listed in this chapter can produce this response.

CHANGES IN EATING HABITS

This can include anything from the cat refusing to eat at all to eating more than usual. If your cat refuses to eat and a physical exam has ruled out any possibility of illness or mouth problems, then finding the cause of the cat's stress is imperative. Talk to your veterinarian about the best course of action to get your cat eating properly. (See Chapter Ten for more information on diet for the indoor cat.)

CHEWING

A cat that suddenly eats your plants when before they were left alone, or that develops a taste for inedible objects (such as a blanket or your clothes) may be showing a stress-related behavior. She may also have a medical problem, so be sure to have her checked by your veterinarian.

AGGRESSION

This may include aggression toward other cats or people. A cat under stress may begin to attack other cats for apparently no reason, bite, claw and growl. While I mentioned earlier that little cat spats are nothing to worry about, aggression from stress is different from other types of normal feline aggression, such as playful aggression (when two cats or kittens are mock-fighting, there will be little or no growling and claws will not be fully extended) or petting aggression (some cats will only tolerate being petted for so long, then will bite or claw at your hand to let you know they have had enough).

Some cats, particularly feral cats or cats that lack proper socialization, will be aggressive to some extent as part of their personality. Aggression is a sign of stress only if it comes on suddenly or is the result of a change in the cat's life.

Aggression can also be a sign that something physical is wrong. Often when a cat does not feel well, she will show her discomfort by aggressively protecting the area that is painful. A trip to the vet can rule out a physical ailment.

DISPLACED AGGRESSION

Dogs and wolves are not the only animals to form pack hierarchies. In a multi-cat household, the cats must also form a type of order that tells each cat in the household who's on what level in the pack. This is true even when you have just two cats.

If a higher-ranking cat is picking on a lesser cat, the lesser cat many times will take her frustration out on a cat even lower in the hierarchy. This is called displaced or redirected aggression. It frequently occurs when a new cat is brought into the household and temporarily upsets the established order, and generally works itself out over time. But if you're seeing displaced aggression in a well-established group, you need to find out exactly what the problem is.

FEAR

Stress can also be the cause of fear or shyness in cats. Any of the stressors mentioned in this chapter can cause a fear reaction in a cat. Fear itself can also cause stress. A fearful cat will display any number of the signs of stress already mentioned.

Often a fearful cat will show aggression towards another cat, or even her owner. A frightened cat will hide and, if forced to come out, will show her reluctance by attacking. Displaced aggression can result with lesser cats in the pecking order, who may grow fearful if the top cat is bullying or intimidating.

Calming the fearful cat will require patience and understanding. In severe cases, a pet behaviorist can be called in to help solve the problem (as well as other behavioral problems and stressors). Speak with your veterinarian about possible medications and treatments to calm the cat's nerves, as well. But remember that medication is, at best, a short-term solution; directly addressing your cat's stress is the long-term answer.

The Inevitable

Most cats are innately fearful of a dip in water or learn to fear going to the vet. You will need much patience and caution when these things are required for your cat.

Stress Relievers

Finding and eliminating the specific cause of your cat's stress is the first major step to take when you see signs of stress, but there are other steps you can also take to prevent or lessen your cat's general stress level.

GOOD NUTRITION

It is vital that all cats be fed a good diet that is 100 percent nutritionally complete for cats (see Chapter Ten for more on diet). However, at times when stress levels may be elevated, a proper diet blended with a veterinarian-recommended vitamin supplement may help to reduce the effects of stress in your cat.

EXERCISE

During stressful times, as with humans, a cat may be lethargic or appear down. Exercise is a proven stress reliever, so during stressful times add some extra playtime with your cat. Regular exercise also helps prevent stress from building up under normal circumstances.

It also helps to keep the cat's weight down (obesity may stress the cat's body, thus making the cat more lethargic and vulnerable to further stress). Cats love to chase objects. Throwing a ball for your cat is a good form of exercise, for yourself as well as your cat. Pounce loves to chase balls, and, unlike most cats, will even bring them back if the ball is spongy enough for him to grip in his mouth.

COMPANIONSHIP

One cat or two? Two cats will be twice the trouble, right? Not necessarily. Two cats, particularly kittens or adult cats that know one another and are proven to get along, will not only take some of the burden off you, but will also prevent some types of stress.

There will be an added vet bill and the litter box will need cleaning a bit more often, but the benefits for the cats will far outweigh the negatives.

Obtaining two cats will also help prevent an only cat from developing King-of-the-House syndrome, which can occur when a cat is raised alone. Dominant cats see a need to keep peace in their community, and once another cat breaks the boundaries, trouble can ensue. A cat that grows from kittenhood to adulthood alone often will not tolerate another cat being brought in later on. Cats can become very jealous, and an only cat will sometimes even resent the introduction of another person (baby or adult) into what the cat sees as her home. This, too, can cause behavioral problems because the cat sees this new introduction as an intruder who is taking the cat's human away.

Two cats raised together will have one another for company. They will play together and sleep together, even groom one another. This leaves you a little more freedom to go out more often and not feel guilty about the cat being home alone. However, this does not mean the cats will need nothing from you; cats love their humans and, even with other cats to play with, they still require and thrive on love from the person who cares for them. The relationship between two cats is a very different one from the relationship between cat and human, and both are beneficial not only to the cats but to you.

SPACE

Cats don't require as much space as some pets, but they still need some room to run and play. Crowding among cats can also cause stress, so be sure you have enough room to meet each cat's individual needs.

COMMUNICATION

Good communication between you and your cat is essential in order to know when something is amiss. Know your cat's body language and usual activity level, what toys are her favorites and how she normally behaves when she's happy. Communicating with your cat also helps form a bond between you that can help to reduce stress for the cat as well as yourself.

ATTENTION AND LOVE

Never underestimate the healing power of love. Provide your cat with plenty of attention, toys, games and TLC. Try to set a time every day to hold, pet and play with your cat (or each cat in your care). Even if your cat seems shy, she needs attention (maybe even more so), so spend time with her and let her come out of her shell through your loving care.

Don't be afraid to use baby talk with your cat. Cats particularly enjoy soft, high voices. Whenever I baby-talk my cats, they begin to purr and squint their eyes, a sign of contentment. They sense and know I love them—they can feel it and they respond accordingly.

INTERACTION, TOYS AND GAMES

My cat Pounce has a simple rule concerning play: "If it moves, pounce on it. If it doesn't move, make it move, then pounce on it."

Cats need to interact and play. Many cats, such as Pounce, make their own games, their own fun. Others need to be enticed. Catnip, bird feeders outside the windows, scratching trees, toys and kitty greens are all essential elements to an indoor cat's well-being.

Be careful which toys you choose for your cat. Simply because a toy is offered for sale does not guarantee it is safe for your cat. *Know your cat* is the first rule in knowing which are the best toys to provide for her entertainment. If your cat is an avid chewer (kittens often fall into this category), try to avoid toys that have string, wire or small pieces that can come off and get lodged in the cat's throat or digestive tract.

Feathers can make great interactive toys.

Make up games and experiment until you find which games your cat enjoys most, then set aside time each day to play these games. Some cats will enjoy obstacle courses to run, soap bubbles to chase or just a rolled up ball of foil to bat around. Interactive toys, such as a feather or toy mouse on a string (and fishing pole–type toys) are fabulous for keeping a cat's muscles in tone.

The Bouncing Game

Quite by accident one day I discovered a game my cats adore. I found a small rubber ball I'd bought years before to use for hand exercises when I'm writing. Rather than simply squeezing the ball, I decided to add a little fun to my routine and started bouncing it on a bare patch of the floor. Before I knew it I was surrounded by five or six cats, their heads bobbing up and down in synchronized movement as they watched the ball go up and come down. Every now and then a paw would jut out at the ball as it hit the floor, but it was always too quick to be caught. Still, they love watching and trying to catch it.

Cats love to play in paper bags.

Shadow is funny; he loves to run up me as if I were a tree and perch on my shoulder. This is a game he developed on his own and he enjoys it. Of course, if I'm wearing shorts or a thin shirt it can be painful, but generally we both get a kick out of it.

Try not to get your cat into the habit of playing with your hands. This can cause the cat to associate scratching and biting hands with play and enjoyment—never a good idea.

MASSAGE

Ahh—massage! Who doesn't love the relaxing effects of a good rubdown? Cats, too, can benefit from massage, not only for its stress-relieving qualities, but because a massage also gives you the chance to check your cat for any lumps, scabs or physical abnormalities.

Most cats will readily accept a massage, so long as it is done when the cat is in the mood to be petted and rubbed. A cat will usually let you know when she has had enough either by getting vocal, suddenly scratching (as some cats will do) or by simply walking away. But most cats will enjoy the massage as long as you keep going.

Giving a cat a massage involves a little more than a simple petting. Using your thumbs, carefully rub the cat, starting with her head, in light, slow circular motions. Working at the animal's muscles, work your way down to the neck, back, legs and paws. Some cats will enjoy it so much they may roll over for you to rub their belly.

Just as with petting, massage will relieve your own stress as well as your cat's.

A good massage can be really relaxing!
(Natalie Chapman)

CATNIP

We all know the effects catnip can have on our cats. A member of the mint family, catnip relaxes cats and gives them a safe, nonaddictive buzz. The chemical responsible for this reaction is called nepetalactone, and it

works through the cat's sense of smell. The scent stimulates certain nerves in the cat's brain, resulting in a cat that is relaxed enough to either get crazy or sleep soundly, depending on the cat.

Not all cats are affected by catnip, however. Young kittens also are not affected.

MUSIC

Yes, music! Soft, classical music or even a radio playing very low can keep your cat(s) company and help relax them when you are not home. Avoid heavy, driving, loud music—though I personally love it, cats don't.

Sammy is the music lover among my cats. Whenever I sit down to play my piano, no matter where Sammy is in the house he will suddenly appear beside me on the piano bench, purring above the music. He will rub against the keys (at times creating music even better than what I am playing) and occasionally touch a paw to a key I just played. I am just waiting for the day when I hear *Für Elise* coming from my piano when I am not at it.

Special Situations

Special situations are those cats with physical limitations such as illness, blindness, deafness or a crippling deformity. These cats may experience a higher level of stress due to their handicap. Cats like these need special care and love. However, conventional stress-reduction methods may not work as well with these cats, so alternative methods must be developed to ease and reduce any stress.

My blind cat, Teisha, for example, cannot play as the other cats do because she can't see a string or a ball to chase. I had to stimulate her other senses in getting her to participate in play sessions. I use catnip toys that make her frisky, and I also use balls with bells in them for her to follow. She will occasionally chase another cat by following the sound of her paws.

If you have a special-situation cat, get to know what things the cat will respond to and use that knowledge to create play events for your particular cat. With plenty of fun activity and love, your cat should feel less stressed and will live a longer and happier life.

The Cat-Friendly Home

Obviously, owning a cat will mean certain changes in your home; cat trees adorning the living room, sofas covered by towels, and cat beds and toys blanketing the floor. But, besides the basics, there are other things you can do to make your home fun and friendly for your cat. Remember, you are creating your cat's entire world. With a little thought and ingenuity, that world can be heaven for your cats.

The following are just a few fun ideas that will make your home more cat-friendly.

What is it that cats like to do (besides eating, scratching and sleeping)? They play, hide and climb. Cats prefer a high vantage point from which to view their domain. Sure, your cats have that wonderful tall cat tree to sit on top of, but that's only one vantage point. Rather than placing a huge cat tree in every room, ramps and perches can be made using a little imagination and skill.

Wooden ramps can be built that lead up walls or onto the counter. At Kitty Angels Humane Society, ramps run up and down the walls of the outdoor enclosure.

I built this playhouse using cardboard boxes and Elmers glue.

Does your cat like to sit on top of the refrigerator? Stairs or a ramp built to the side of the fridge make a wonderful and fun way for your cat to get to one of her favorite spots. Carpeting these ramps not only gives the cat a good grip, but provides an extra scratching area. These ramps can be built along walls in any room or in only one room. I've seen ramps that run from one room to the next. A hole in the wall conveniently placed makes it easy for the cat to get from one room to another without ever having to touch the floor. The choice is yours, and the type of ramps you build and where are limited only by your imagination.

Cabinets are great places for little furry bodies to hide, but you don't want your cat getting into the cabinets that house your cleaning supplies and chemicals. A box or cabinet can be constructed specifically for your cat using either cardboard or wood. (If wood is used, be careful with nails. It's better to use a non-toxic glue.)

I once built a kitty castle using several durable cardboard boxes. I cut cat-sized holes in various places in each box, then strategically glued them together so that one box led to the next. I painted the whole house and placed towels in the bottom of each box. I even built a little open courtyard on one side. If you use sturdy enough cardboard, you can even carpet the whole thing. To attract the cats to it, I attached toys on strings and hung them outside the doors, then placed toys inside.

THE KITTY STAMPEDE

Living in a house with 12 cats, I'm accustomed to the kitty stampede, which generally takes place about two or three o'clock in the morning. As I sit working at my computer (which is located right next to the basement stairs), my concentration will invariably be interrupted around that time by the roaring sound of kitty feet pounding down the stairs at top speed. Distracted, I'll look up to see two or three blurs of various colors whizzing by my desk. I'm used to this, and I know better than to get back to work right away because those same blurred colors, now reversed in position, will whiz by once more and back up the stairs. This is usually followed by some loud banging noise and is my cue to go up and see what was just knocked to the floor.

Cats love to run, and it will be in your cat's best interest as well as your valuables' if you provide space for them to do so. If you have a hallway, great, but my cats prefer the stairs. Wherever your cat likes to run, make sure the way is clear and free of anything breakable.

CHAPTER FOUR

Bathroom Duty

Not too long ago, we had a couple to our home who had never visited before. When I mentioned exactly how many cats were in the house, the woman looked shocked. She sniffed the air. "It doesn't smell like there are 12 cats here," she said. I took that as a compliment.

Probably the most unenjoyable yet necessary aspect of indoor cat ownership is litter box duty. As mundane a subject as litter and litter boxes may seem, it's an important one not only for your cat, but for you as well. Your indoor cat relies on you, and since she no longer has all of outdoors to choose as a bathroom, it's your duty to provide a place that will satisfy her instincts and allow her to continue to go where she feels most comfortable going.

You are the one who must decide where the litter box is placed, what type of litter to use, what kind of litter box is best for your cat(s), how many boxes you should have and what to do if your cat stops using the litter box. And then there's that most dreadful of subjects: cleaning the box!

Indoor cat owners generally accept this most unpleasant of duties (they love their cats!) and constantly strive for new and better ways to rid their houses of that odoriferous scent that can perfume the air each time kitty uses the box.

Before it was widely known that cats could survive happily indoors, most cats never even saw a litter box. The rare times when they were kept indoors, due to bad weather or some other temporary reason, they had to make do with a box, usually wooden, filled with sand or ash. These fillers did little to neutralize odors and were not always the most absorbent and easily cleaned materials.

But in 1947 an event occurred that would shape the yet-to-come cat-box filler industry: Kitty Litter, the first publicly marketed cat-box filler, was discovered quite by accident. Edward Lowe, who at the time worked for his father's industrial supply company, was visited by his neighbor, who asked him if he had any sand she could use for her cat's box. The weather was cold and the sand Lowe had outside was frozen, so he gave her a bag of granulated clay to try. She used the clay and then remarked to Lowe how it was wonderfully absorbent and easy to clean. This gave Lowe an idea. He filled some bags with the clay, called them Kitty Litter and marketed his products, first locally then at cat shows. Kitty Litter was a huge success.

Litter Box Fillers

Since 1947 hundreds of different types and brands of cat-box filler have been marketed. Go to any pet supply or grocery store and you will be faced with a bewildering variety of choices.

Just as every cat is different, so is every litter and every cat's litter preference. Cats are clean, picky creatures, and some cats will refuse to use certain litters for reasons that may or may not be obvious to their owners. For example, declawed cats, particularly right after surgery, may avoid certain litters that may hurt their now-sensitive feet. But with the variety of litters available, often one can be found that will be to your cat's liking.

CLAY LITTER

Not only are clay litters inexpensive, they are one of the most widely available cat litters on the market. At one time, traditional clay litter was the only type available commercially, and the only odor control ingredient used by cat owners was baking soda sprinkled on the top of the litter. Now clay litter is available in many different varieties, from unscented natural to ones that incorporate odor crystals and deodorants.

The two drawbacks most often mentioned about clay litter is that it tends to be tracked around the house, and that the clay can be dusty, which may irritate some cats. Tracking can be reduced by putting a carpet remnant at the entrance to the litter box. Some companies now also sell mats that help clean litter off a cat's feet as she exits the box. Dust-free clay litters are now available, too.

Another disadvantage to traditional clay litters is that they are not always best for the multi-cat household. Even the ones with the most odor-absorbing compounds cannot always keep up in a household with several cats. And while solid wastes should be scooped from all litter boxes every day, traditional clay litters do not allow the removal of urea. Therefore, the box must be dumped and the litter changed every three to five days, depending on the number of cats in your household. If you have only one or two cats, however, clay litter can be a great choice, particularly for someone on a limited budget.

CLUMPING CLAY LITTER

Nine out of 10 cats agree, clumping litter is the way to go. Developed around 1984 by a biochemist named Thomas Nelson, almost half of all litter sales today are clumping cat litters. These litters are treated with chemicals that cause the clay to bond when moistened. The cat owner can then simply scoop the clump from the box, leaving no urine or odors behind.

Like traditional clay litters, the clumping varieties are available in many different types, including low dust, low tracking, multi-cat, deodorized and natural. Clumping litters are great for households with many cats and allow for the prompt removal of clumped urea.

The texture of clumping clay litters is more like sand than other forms of litters, and is therefore widely accepted by most cats. This litter is a bit more expensive than traditional clay, but since it does not need to be emptied and replaced as often, the cost in the long run ends up about the same.

Does removing the clumps mean you never have to dump the litter and replace it completely? No. Germs can still adhere to the litter box, so for your cat's health the box should be dumped and cleaned, and the litter replaced at least every few weeks.

There has been some controversy over whether or not clumping litters can form clumps in a cat's stomach and intestinal tract after the cat has licked it from her paws. Experts recommend not using clumping litters with kittens under four months of age. For adult cats, however, there should be no problem. Usually the amount of litter left on a cat's paws after she steps from the box, walks across the floor and then stops to clean herself is so small that no health problems result from swallowing a bit of it.

Tracking also seems to be a complaint about clumping litters, but now there are reduced tracking litters available. These litters have a larger grain, which helps reduce the amount of litter trapped between a cat's toes.

Certain clumping litters, if not scooped constantly, can form cement-like clumps that adhere to the bottom of the box. These are difficult to remove after they have been allowed to build up. When buying clumping litter, it is best to experiment and find the brand you and your cat prefer.

WOOD CHIPS

These can include chips, sawdust and shavings. Cedar and pine are the most common woods used for these types of litters. Litters with a cedar base are very odor absorbent, and wood-based litters are environmentally friendly. Although wood litters, particularly cedar, can be used well in multi-cat situations, they, like traditional clay, need to be replaced and the box cleaned more often than with the clumping litters.

CORNCOB

Because corncob litter is made from a product that is normally considered food, most people don't think of it as suitable for a litter box—might the cats eat it instead? But companies that manufacture corncob litters claim it is milled in a way that makes it unappealing to the palate.

And if cats were to eat it, the litter would simply pass through their digestive tract with no difficulty.

Corncob litter is milled by separating the cobs into two parts, light and heavy. The parts are then ground up, heated and made into pellets, which are then ground again and put through a filtering process.

Besides being biodegradable and flushable, corncob litters are highly absorbent and appealing to most cats.

NEWSPAPER

While shredded newspaper is sometimes recommended for cats immediately after declawing, it is not suitable for long-term litter box use. Instead, there is a litter for the eco-conscious person made from recycled newspaper. This litter is put through a process that binds the ink so it will not come off on the cat's paws or be tracked through your house. In small quantities, this litter is flushable and absorbent.

If your cat has recently had surgery (particularly declawing or other surgeries involving her feet), this litter is soft and lightweight, and therefore more gentle on sensitive feet.

GRASS

Bales of straw and grasses are chopped up and ground into small pieces, which are then put through a pelleting process, to manufacture these litters. The process prevents them from falling apart when moistened. Grass litter is eco-friendly and absorbent, and tends to control urea odors better than traditional clay litters.

CITRUS PEELS, GRAINS, WHEAT AND PEANUT SHELLS

These litters, most of which are considered food rather than litter, are also eco-friendly. Citrus cat litters are made from recycled fruit wastes, generally the peels from dejuiced citrus fruits. They are cooked at a high temperature to kill off bacteria, and the dust is cleaned out through a filtering process. The residual acids on the fruit peels help to reduce and neutralize the ammonia smell in the cat's urine, almost completely eliminating odors.

Grain and wheat litters are made in much the same way as pet foods. Gluten in grain litters helps make them clumpable. These litters are also flushable and can actually be good for a septic system by adding enzymes.

Peanut shell litter, grain and wheat litter are all edible, as well. So if kitty decides to make a snack out of her litter, there will be no harmful effects.

MAKING YOUR CHOICE

So many choices make buying litter sound confusing. But the up side is that there is enough variety to ensure that every cat will be happy.

Sometimes litters can be mixed to offer the owner the advantages of one litter and the cat the advantages of another. My cats, for instance, prefer the clumping litters, and I like the ease of cleaning them. But with some of my cats, the odor-controlling properties of these are not always enough. I remedied this situation by filling the box with clumping litter and placing a soft cedar litter as a top layer. (I keep the layer thin so it doesn't interfere with the clumping properties of the clay.) The cedar masks the odors until I can scoop the box, and the urine is still easily removed with the clumps.

Your best bet is to experiment and find out which litter or combination of litters is most preferred by you and your cat. Your cat will let you know what she does and doesn't like. The most common way to send this message is simply to refuse to use the box. Dissatisfied cats will often eliminate on the floor near the box.

Litter Boxes

With all the choices of litter box fillers available, you need something to put them in. There are almost as many types and styles of litter boxes as there are litters. What box you choose will depend on you and your cat.

WHAT KIND OF BOX?

What kind of litter box is right for your cat? The answer will depend on your cat, your preference, the room available and where the box (or boxes) will be placed.

For kittens, it is probably best to start out with a smaller, open box and get a larger one when the cat grows big enough for it. A large box for a small kitten is not a good idea. A kitten that continuously has to struggle to climb into the box may decide the effort is not worth it and start doing her business in other locations.

Many styles of boxes are designed with ease of cleaning in mind. Some companies sell boxes with one or more parts where the litter is sifted

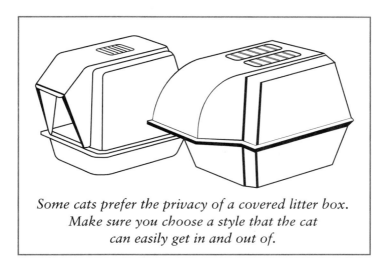

*Some cats prefer the privacy of a covered litter box.
Make sure you choose a style that the cat
can easily get in and out of.*

from one box to the next and the solid waste is discarded. Although they can be used with almost any litter type, these litter boxes work best with clumping litters.

Some people prefer covered litter boxes. These give kitty a private place to go, help keep odors from spreading throughout the house, and keep litter spills to a minimum—a real concern if your cat likes to scratch a lot in the litter.

While some cats prefer the privacy, others will not use them. I am not sure if cats can be labeled claustrophobic, but some cats definitely have an aversion to stepping through a tiny hole to do their duty (these same cats may also hate the confines of a carrier, so perhaps they are claustrophobic).

If you choose to use a covered box and your cat accepts it, be sure you don't forget to scoop every day. Because the odors are kept within the box for the most part and the dirty litter is not as obvious as with an open box, it can be easy to forget that the box needs to be cleaned just as regularly. Many cats will not go in a dirty box and will let you know when the box is simply too dirty for them by leaving you a "reminder" somewhere else in the house.

Every cat is different when it comes to litter box cleanliness. Some will tolerate a fair bit, but I know of several cats that will not go in a litter box that is even slightly soiled. Instead, they will go on the floor beside the box.

Boxes are also available with plastic lips around the edge that fold in and help prevent litter from spilling or being tossed out as the cat scratches. Again, make sure your cat will use this type of box and can easily get in and out of it.

Self-cleaning boxes are now also available. These litter boxes work by sifting the litter mechanically and pushing it into a tray that can be removed and dumped easily. Clumping litters are the best choice to use with these boxes, as the mechanism can only remove clumps of material. While cats will love the cleanliness of such a box, some will not like the movement and mechanical sounds it makes.

Dry system litter boxes come equipped with an aeration system and replaceable pads that absorb and dry urine before odors can develop. They must be used with a special type of rock litter that is periodically washed. These systems are available through some pet supply catalogs and retailers.

Regardless of the type of box you choose, make sure it is one your cat will be able and willing to use, and is not too big or too small for the size cat you have.

Where to Put It?

Most cats, like humans, prefer a little privacy when performing certain tasks. The decision where to place your cat's litter box should be based on this fact, as well as the space available in your home, accessibility for the cat, convenience and your personal preference.

Putting the litter box in a basement (or other room) your cat rarely frequents will probably result in a mess elsewhere, particularly during stressful times or if the cat has an upset in her bowels due to illness or something she ate. If, however, your cat spends much of her time carousing for spiders (or whatever else she enjoys) in the basement, then placing the litter box there is not a bad idea.

If you have the room, and particularly if you have more than one cat, you may want two or more litter boxes in various locations throughout the house. If you have more than three cats, you will definitely want to buy more than one litter box and place them in various locations around the house. Having four or more cats with only one litter box can be too trying on the nerves (yours and your cats'), as the box will have to be scooped and cleaned continuously throughout the day.

The bathroom is the most frequent, and obvious, location for a litter box. Usually bathrooms are quiet and out of the way of heavy traffic (unless you are having a party—then kitty can be placed, litter box and all, in a room away from the noise), and if you use a flushable litter, cleaning the box is simplified.

It's important to remember that, regardless of where you choose to place the box, it should be in an area free from excessive noise and movement, and away from where the cat eats and sleeps. But it must be in a location the cat can get to easily and willingly.

There are many ways to hide a litter box creatively and still allow the cat to find it conveniently. The box can be placed under a sink (provided there is enough room, easy access for the cat, no harmful chemicals nearby and your cat knows where to find the box). Most pet supply companies sell attractive screens specifically made to place around a litter box.

With a little imagination and carpentry skills, you can build a cabinet or shelter for the box. If you do, make sure to allow plenty of room for the cat and box and an easily accessible opening not only for the cat but for removal of the box. Also, it's a good idea to place a hole in the side where you can fasten a screen, or provide some other way for the odor to escape. Otherwise the odors may permeate and ruin the cat box shelter, and some cats will refuse to use it if it smells.

Children love sandboxes to play in, and to some children, the cat box is the best—an indoor sand box always available for their enjoyment. The best solution to this problem is to put the litter box where the child cannot get to it. This can be a cabinet or a separate room with the door kept closed to keep the child out. Of course, if you do this, you must find a way for the cat to get in the room, but not the child. Many stores and catalogs offer cat doors for sale, or you can build one yourself.

I have seen many imaginative and interesting things done with cat boxes to hide them from human view. You can easily try any number of things, keeping in mind the ease of cleaning and accessibility to the cat. Or you can do what I do: Simply place open cat boxes in

Litter Box Liners

Litter box liners can be used to help keep odors from adhering to the box and help with cleaning. Rather than dumping the litter when it becomes soiled, a litter liner allows you to simply lift the entire "package" right out of the box.

Cats rarely scratch only the litter, however. They also get the side of the box, the wall behind the box and even the floor. Cats with all claws intact usually tear liners when they scratch, spilling litter back into the box and defeating the purpose of the liner.

Most people choose to line their boxes with newspaper, which can aid in cleaning and prevent litter from sticking to the bottom of the box. But, as with liners, cats will eventually rip newspapers to shreds.

various locations, making no attempt to hide them at all (and keeping them *extra* clean). But, whichever location you choose for the litter box, make sure your cat knows where it is by bringing her to the box.

Maintenance and Odor Control

Some people refuse to talk about it, others simply shrug and pretend it's no big deal, and still others are embarrassed by the subject. I'm talking about the most important task in litter box duty—cleaning. But as unappealing as this task is, it's a necessity for your cat's health and to keep your home odor-free. I think if cats could philosophize, the most popular philosophy they would come up with is that one can never be too clean when it comes to litter boxes.

When placing litter in the box, try not to put in too much or too little. Too much litter is harder to clean as the urine seeps to the bottom (and will also add to the spillage), and too little will need to be cleaned constantly. I usually fill my litter boxes close to half full, and I scoop each box (we have five) twice a day.

Odors are caused by bacteria, and bacteria is everywhere. Just scooping the litter box is not enough to keep these microscopic creatures out

There is just no substitute for frequent scooping.

and away from your cat and home. The box needs to be emptied completely and the litter changed every few days with traditional, non-clumping litters and approximately once a month with clumping litters. The box should also be washed every time you change the litter, using an antibacterial detergent that is safe for pets. Pet supply stores carry many brands of cleaning agents that neutralize odors and will not make your cat ill with harmful odors or ingredients.

You can use a diluted bleach solution to clean the box more thoroughly once every month or two if you feel the odors are building up within the box (remember that plastic is porous and tends to hold smells). But be careful. Bleach is harmful to cats if they breathe it in or lick it from the box or their paws. Make sure the bleach is thoroughly rinsed from the box before refilling it with litter (a good test is that if you can smell the bleach, so can your cat).

After many years of keeping saltwater fish and, on occasion, bleaching coral, I have learned that a good way to get rid of bleach odors is to place the item in the sun, allowing the heat to bake the bleach out. You can do this with litter boxes, too. After rinsing as thoroughly as possible, place the empty litter box in the sunshine for the day. When you can no longer smell even the slightest trace of bleach, rinse the box again (you can never be too safe), dry it and refill it. It's good idea when you do this to have a backup litter box to use while the other one is sunning.

Keeping the litter dry is another way to help prevent odors and bacteria from multiplying. Scooping two or three times a day will keep the litter sifted, helping it to stay dry. Make sure, however, that when you scoop, you get to the bottom of the box. And after washing the box out, dry it thoroughly before refilling it with litter. You don't want to trap moisture beneath the litter before the cat even uses it.

Sometimes, regardless of what you do or how well you clean the box, after a while it simply gets too dirty to be cleaned. Plastic is porous, and eventually bacteria seeps in and ruins the box. If you can, replace the litter box every year or two, helping to keep your cat's are a fresh.

A good habit to get into, and one that I follow daily, is to keep an eye on the contents of the litter box as you scoop. This way, if there is any problem, such as bloody urine or diarrhea, you will spot it before it gets out of hand and can take steps to find out which cat may be ill or get a stool sample to the veterinarian.

Even if you keep your cat's box exceptionally clean, there may still be the occasional accident. A cat that has a bowel or bladder problem may not be able to hold it long enough to get to the box, or may run or drip. To clean up these accidents and control their odors, it is best to get to them as soon as they are made. This is not always possible, but the sooner you get to the mess (especially with urine), the better your chance will be of cleaning it efficiently. If urine is allowed to soak into any surface (particularly carpets), there is a greater chance the cat will reuse that area as its toilet, or another cat may use the same spot. Use an enzymatic cleaner and let it soak into the carpet. The enzymes will break down the urine, removing the "food" that bacteria feed on. Odor neutralizers are also available that can be used to clean the area, and sprays can kill odors in a specific spot.

The idea is to get rid of the smell, not cover it up. Cats have very sensitive olfactory nerves and can smell the urine even beneath some of the strongest-smelling products. For that reason, avoid cleaning up accidents with ammonia because its lingering scent smells a lot like cat urine.

My Cleanup Solution

When my cats have an accident, I spot clean the area by first soaking it with a diluted solution of deodorizing cleaner. Then I soak up the liquid with a towel and scrub using a stiff-bristled brush (not too stiff—you don't want to dig up the carpet). If a stain is still there, I use Resolve Carpet Cleaner or Woolite Pet Stain Eliminator. To help the area dry, I usually will sprinkle the spot with baking soda, let it sit for a day, then brush it with a dry brush to loosen the particles and vacuum. (See Chapter Six for more on keeping your carpets and house clean.)

Litter Box Problems

My cat Candy, a spayed female, is fastidious about using the litter box—except when a new cat comes into the house. Suddenly she begins eliminating on the counters and occasionally on the carpet in the living room. This behavior usually lasts a few months, until the new cat is comfortably integrated into the hierarchy of the household cats and takes on the familiar scent of the house.

Territorial marking, as Candy occasionally exhibits, is only one of the many reasons a cat may suddenly stop using her litter box. Refusal to use the box, or occasional lapses for the normally fastidious cat, is the number one behavioral problem in cats and one of the biggest reasons cats are given away to shelters. At some point in their lives, 10 percent of all cats develop a problem associated with the litter box.

Finding the reason a cat is not using her litter box, or why she has suddenly stopped using it, can be a challenge. The very first step to take is a trip to the veterinarian. Often cats with a physical problem, such as a urinary tract disorder, will begin to associate the discomfort they feel from the illness with the litter box, because of the pain that's present whenever they climb into the box to relieve themselves. This sudden negative association with their litter box can make them decide the box is the cause of their troubles, and is best avoided.

If a visit to the vet rules out any physical problem, you will have to do a little detective work. If your cat has suddenly decided she would rather relieve herself on your Persian carpet than in her box, think about why and try to eliminate the problem. Here are a few of the more common reasons a cat may stop using her box.

THE BOX ITSELF

This can include the size of the box, the style of box or even the material the box is made from. Some cats have problems with covered boxes or the odd shape of self-cleaning boxes, so if you have recently purchased one and your cat refuses to use it, you have basically two choices: (1) Get rid of the box and go back to using the tried-and-true version you had before; (2) Try to retrain the cat to use the box. This involves showing the cat that there is nothing to fear from this new device by bringing her to the box gently and showing her the box. Speak in a soothing tone of voice and do not hold the cat there if she wishes to run away. If you show the cat often enough that this box is not going to harm her, she may soon be using it the way she did the old box.

Cats may also be picky about the material the box is made out of. Commercial litter boxes are almost always made from a hard, durable plastic that is accepted by cats. But I have seen some people who make litter boxes out of other items such as pans, boxes (wood or cardboard) and other materials which may or may not be acceptable to the cat or easily cleanable by the owner. If the litter box is made of a material that seems strange to the cat (either by its smell or its feel beneath her paws), she may reject it. In any case, a litter box should be made of a material that is easy to clean because, as mentioned above, cats often will not use a box that they consider dirty or smelly.

TYPE OF LITTER

Certain deodorizing litters or sprinkle-on deodorizers can irritate some cats' nasal passages and even their feet. This may cause them to avoid the litter box altogether and use an area more familiar, such as your carpet. Try a plain low-dust cat litter and no deodorizers as an alternative.

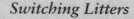

> ## Switching Litters
>
>
>
> Cats don't usually enjoy changes to their environment, and I have found that occasionally switching litters will cause some of my cats to avoid the box. To remedy this problem, I gradually add more and more of the new litter to the old litter over a period of days or even weeks, allowing the cats to slowly adjust to the new litter. However, you may have to stick with your old litter if your cat simply will not accept a change.

NEW CAT, NEW LOCATION

A new cat in the house may not know right away where the litter box is. That's why it is imperative to show the cat where the litter box is several times a day for the first few days (see Chapter Two for more on introducing a new cat into your home).

Changing the location of the litter box can also cause confusion. If the litter box is normally kept in the bathroom and later it is moved to the hallway, often the cat will continue to use the area where the litter box once was. In a case like this, it will be necessary not only to show the cat where the litter box is now kept, just as you would with a new cat, but you will also have to make the place where the box used to be unattractive to the cat (the section "Training and Retraining" later in this chapter will explain how).

DECLAWING

Surgery to remove a cat's claws is a process that leaves the paws sensitive, making litter seem too rough and painful. Often, when a cat returns from this surgery she will refuse to use the litter box. Using a softer litter may help, but occasionally the cat will continue to fear the box even after her paws have healed.

Sometimes moving the location of the litter box or adding a new litter box will help. If not, retraining the cat to use her box and to re-associate the box with something positive will be required (see "Training and Retraining"). Shredded newspapers or litters made from recycled newspaper should be used for two weeks after declaw surgery, as they are easier on sensitive feet.

Territorial Disputes

This mostly takes the form of urine spraying, which can be done either in the usual squatting position or by backing up to a vertical surface such as the wall. Marking is an instinctual behavior. In the wild, cats mark out an area that they consider theirs. This is communication; the cat is leaving an odoriferous message that tells other cats to stay away from that area.

Cats also mark when they feel their territory is threatened or invaded by another cat. Just because a cat is kept indoors does not always mean this instinctual behavior will be eliminated. In a case like this, simply marking in the litter box is not enough to a cat. The cat may not even know why she is marking, but just feels that she *must*.

New people, odors and other cats or animals can make a territorial cat feel she needs to redefine her own particular location. A cat may even spray an object or piece of clothing that smells unfamiliar or smells of another cat.

A cat that has come of age (about six months old) and has not yet been altered, a cat that is in heat or a male cat that senses a female cat nearby may spray to show other cats "this is my turf." Usually having a male cat neutered before any of this behavior begins, or a female spayed before her first heat, can prevent this type of spraying later in the cat's life. But on occasion even some altered cats may spray. Usually once the perceived threat has passed, the behavior will pass, too.

Fear

A fearful cat may suddenly stop using her litter box. If something happened near the box to frighten the cat, she will see the box as the source of her fear and will not want to go near it.

A shy cat or a cat bullied by another cat may feel on guard at all times and will not want to venture too far to reach a crowded litter box. A cat like this should have her own litter box placed near the area where she spends most of her time.

STRESS

In Chapter Three I discussed the many reasons indoor cats may become stressed, and I don't need to repeat that information here. But it is important to remember that stress is one of the most major factors involved in litter box lapses.

JEALOUSY

This goes hand in hand with stress. A new baby in the house that takes up the attention you used to give the cat is a common cause of jealously. A new marriage or a new pet can also prompt a cat to show her disapproval by eliminating inappropriately. In any new situation in your cat's life, make sure you prepare the cat in advance by introducing her slowly to whatever change is yet to come. For instance, show the cat the baby's things and items associated with a baby before the actual arrival of the infant. Or have your fiancé visit often and interact with the cats. Let him or her leave an item of clothing in your house so the cat will become familiar with the scent.

Sometimes taking a trip will cause a kind of separation anxiety in cats that manifests itself in indiscriminate urination. My stepfather, being a truck driver, is often gone for two or three days at a time. His cat Sylvia (affectionately dubbed Little Girl) will, on occasion, leave him a "reminder" in his overnight bag that she is there and does not want him to leave her. It's a strange way of showing her affection, but it is, in a sense, a feline way of saying, "I love you, don't leave me."

Stray and Feral Cats

Cats that were born, raised or lived a long time outdoors may not know what a litter box is, particularly if they were trained from the start that the ground is their litter box. In this case, a slow but thorough retraining will be essential. A fine-grain, sand-like litter should be used, or you can start out with dirt and work up to litter slowly. With these cats, a clean litter box is extremely important.

COMPETITION

How many cats occupy your house and use the litter boxes? Certain cats will be picky about using a litter box frequented by other cats. You should provide enough litter boxes for the number of cats in the household, based on how well the cats all get along. In my house, some of the cats are not part of the small social hierarchy and are reluctant to use the litter boxes frequented by the cats that are. To remedy this problem, a couple of the cats have separate litter boxes that are, for the most part, used only by them.

Some experts recommend having one litter box per cat. This is fine if you have only two or three cats and want each cat to have her own box. But I have eight cats, and my mother, who lives upstairs, has four cats. That's 12 cats in one household. We have five litter boxes that are kept scooped and cleaned. I believe one box for every two or three cats is sufficient, unless a cat needs to have her own box.

DIRTY BOX

We all know how fastidiously clean cats are. Their sniffers are much more sensitive than ours. And, as has been discussed, some cats refuse to go in a soiled box. See the section "Maintenance and Odor Control" earlier in this chapter for more on keeping the box clean.

LOCATION

The location of the litter box is important. Some cats relish privacy and may choose a remote spot as their bathroom if the litter box is in a high-traffic area.

Also, some cats grow accustomed to the particular location of the box. If the box is moved, the cat may continue to go where the box once was.

If it's necessary to move the box, try moving it just a short distance at a time until it's in its new location, or distract the cat from where the box used to be until she is completely used to the new place.

SIZE

If the box is too small, your cat may feel cramped and uncomfortable inside and need more room. If the box is too large, especially for a young kitten, she may have trouble getting in and out.

LINERS

Some cats simply reject the idea of liners in their boxes. A shy cat may be frightened by the crinkling sound of the liner as she scratches. Newspaper may have similar negative effects.

No one but the cat knows all her reasons for everything she does. Sometimes a cat will suddenly decide, for no apparent reason, that she no longer likes her box or the litter. She will either cease using it altogether or stop one litter box activity and not the other (for example, urinating in the box but defecating on the carpet). To the cat there is a reason for this. But to the owner that reason may seem unfathomable—hidden beneath a veil of unanswered questions.

In severe cases where every possible means has been tried, every possible solution gone over, you may want to talk to your vet about medication for the cat (a temporary solution which may or may not help) or about recommending an animal behavior therapist. Perhaps together you can come up with the answer.

Training and Retraining

Kittens learn litter box etiquette and where to go from their mothers. Through her they learn to bury and cover. The rest is instinct. Even cats that were not trained to use the litter box early on by their mother have shown signs of knowing instinctively how to rake their paws through dirt.

A mother cat usually begins teaching her kittens about the litter box between three and four weeks of age. Generally, when you acquire a kitten, she will be at least six to eight weeks of age or older, so this will already be accomplished, and all you will need to do is remind your new pet where the litter box is the first few days. However, if a younger kitten has fallen into your hands, or if you acquire a kitten who does not seem to know what the litter box is used for, you shall have to step in as a surrogate mother (or father).

Remember, your best chance for success will be to first set up everything to the kitty's liking: proper location, size and type of box, comfortable litter and most of all patience and perseverance.

Kitty will need to be shown the litter box regularly and at times when a kitten (or cat) would normally do her business. The most common times are after naps, playtime and meals, just like a human baby. Set the kitten in the box, and speaking in a soothing tone, carefully and gently move her front paws in a digging motion once or twice. If the kitten begins to sniff around, back away and allow her some privacy. Don't force the kitten to stay in the box if she doesn't wish to. You want to use positive reinforcement rather than a scolding tone that will give the box a negative association. Don't even use something like a squirt gun if the kitten or cat has an accident. All this will do is tell the cat she is doing something wrong by taking care of her natural urges and will only confuse her.

After you've shown your cat the box a few times, she should get the hang of what is supposed to be done there. Continue to show the kitten the box, taking her there regularly and watching for telltale signs that she has the urge to go (sniffing around, scratching, etc.), until the kitten is using the box on her own.

Retraining a cat or kitten that has always used the box but has now stopped may take more time. Success will depend on eliminating

Diapers

As a last resort, if your cat simply refuses to use the litter box or if you are in the process of retraining, you might want to try diapers. Yes, diapers. It sounds strange and looks stranger, but if your cat will wear them, it is preferable to putting the cat down or giving her up.

Cat breeders sometimes use them for their intact males, who will often spray quite a bit in a cattery. I don't mean Huggies or a pinned-on cloth; the diapers best used for a cat are actually heat harnesses/pads for dogs. For most cats, the petite or extra-small sizes work the best.

Some of these are simply material that is fastened around the animal's back end, around the tail. Others are pretty and elaborate—underwear for your pet. Whichever style you choose, you will want something more absorbent than the pads offered for dogs in heat. Maxi pads designed for women work best for absorbing abundant liquid such as urine.

whatever caused the behavior to begin with; retraining will only work if you also remedy the cause of the cat's trouble.

As with training a kitten, retraining should be done with patience, using positive reinforcement. The cat should never be yelled at or scolded, as this may only make matters worse.

You may need to move the location of the litter box for retraining, particularly if the problem was one associated with fear. The location alone may frighten the cat, and putting the box (or better yet, a new box) in a different place may eliminate the problem. A cat that is bullied may need her litter box placed in close proximity to where she spends most of her time (preferably her own box, not to be used by any other cat).

If surgery or an illness was the cause of the cat's refusal to use the box, try a new litter. The different experience may help to break the cat's old association of the litter box with a painful problem. In a case like this, moving or changing the box can also be helpful.

Try placing more than one box in different locations, even if you have only one cat. If you find the cat likes to urinate in the box but defecate elsewhere (or vice versa), try two boxes. One box should be kept in its usual location. The other box you can place where the cat seems to be eliminating most frequently, gradually moving the box until it is where you want it to be. Or you can try placing a small amount of the cat's stool in the new box in the location where you want it. (Only a small amount, though. Remember, cats like cleanliness.) Show the cat the box frequently, speaking soothingly and maybe moving her paws to show her she has a new place to choose. Retrain your cat with frequent trips to the litter box, in much the same way as training a kitten is described previously.

When you're not home to supervise, try confining the cat to a room with her litter box, food and water. A small room is best (I made a small room for one of my cats in an area beneath the stairs) so that the cat will be less likely to use the floor and more likely to use the box. Confinement does not have to be permanent. Once the problem has been eliminated and the cat is using the box regularly, you can try letting the cat out of confinement and see how things go.

Placing your cat's food and water dishes on the spot where she has her accidents (especially if she seems to like one particular location) may help prevent the cat from going back to that area. Cats do not like to eat

Supervision Works

When one of my cats was having litter box problems, I kept her confined only when I was not able to really supervise her. Then I would feed her, wait until she used the litter box, then take her out of confinement. Even after the problem was resolved and I no longer confined her, I would still place her in the litter box myself each time she woke, after she ate and at various times during the day (keeping her confined for shorter and shorter periods of time when I was not home). To this day, unfortunately, I still have to sometimes supervise her litter box activities, but she is no longer kept confined and she is behaving much better.

where they eliminate. Clean the area well before placing the food and water dishes there.

Sometimes you may have to experiment with different methods before finding one that works with your cat. Just remember, however, that cats like to feel comfortable. By simulating as best you can the area a cat would use if she were outside, you have a greater chance of success.

If you have an outdoor cat you are converting to an indoor pet, simulating her outdoor environment is a must. Find a litter that best imitates the surface area the cat likes the most. If you keep the litter box in an out-of-the-way area and your cat insists on going in the kitchen, try moving the box to the kitchen (or placing one box in each location).

Toilet Training

A cat on a toilet? Believe it or not, some people have successfully toilet trained their cats. Pet supply shops and some gift catalogs sell cat toilet-training kits that come with a specially designed seat cover, instructions and herbs attractive to cats. The idea is to place the special seat cover over your toilet seat, so it becomes sort of like a make-shift litter box. Litter is placed inside, and is slowly removed as the cat learns that this is where she is to do her business. Eventually the special seat cover is removed, and the cat eliminates into the toilet—very convenient for the owner.

The sight of a cat squatting over the toilet is quite a humorous one. This method is more successful for the owner of one or two cats, rather than for a house full of cats, and is an interesting substitution for the litter box. Teaching your cat to flush, however, is up to you.

CHAPTER FIVE

The Claws That Scratch

It grates on the nerves like the sound of fingernails across a blackboard—that horrible ripping and tearing of cat claws in your sofa. But don't despair. There is hope, and you don't have to send your cat packing if she decides to use your sofa for a scratching post.

As with anything regarding cats, it's important to understand the reason behind your cat's behavior so you can determine the best methods of controlling it.

Why Cats Scratch

Until she was about four weeks of age, your cat did not even know how to retract her claws. After that, she learned how to use those little tiny needles for a behavior that would one day prove useful in many ways.

Your cat does not scratch the sofa, carpet or drapes (or any other inappropriate area of the house) as some malicious act of spite. She is simply acting out an innate behavior. Cats need to scratch, and there are three good reasons why.

*Cats have scent glands on the sides of their faces
and will rub them against objects to mark territory.
Often, the same object that is rubbed is
also scratched. (Beth Adelman)*

First, scratching removes the outer sheath of the claw, shedding it something like a snake sheds its skin. This sharpens the claws, in a sense. As the hull is stripped away, a new sharper claw is left behind. This keeps the cat's defense capabilities up to maximum and provides the cat with a swift escape from predators. Fortunately for the indoor cat, her most formidable predator is the vacuum cleaner, but the physical structure of the claw remains the same even if the cat does not go outside.

Like urine spraying, scratching is also a form of territory marking. The bottoms of a cat's feet are filled not only with tiny capillaries that dilate and perspire (which helps the cat regulate her body temperature), but also with scent glands. When a cat scratches, she leaves a physical reminder to other cats and a scent marker that clearly states this is her area. Often a cat will touch you with her paws, letting you know that you are her human.

Third, cats scratch to stretch the muscles in their paws, back and legs. Just as humans stretch when they awaken or after sitting for a long time, so do cats. They use their claws to anchor their front half so they can get a good stretch throughout the rest of their body. This is good for the cat's health.

Those are the three most common reasons cats use their claws, but they are used for many other purposes, as well. When your cat was a kitten and still nursing from her mother, she used her tiny paws and little needle-like claws to knead at the teats, which helped stimulate milk flow. As adults, most cats still indulge in kneading behavior when they are content, a throwback to the behavior that gave them such positive results in kittenhood. Unfortunately for us, however, most cats still use their now talon-like claws when kneading, often on your lap.

My cat Sammy loves my long hair. At night, he curls himself up in it as if it were another cat and kneads at the back of my head. Keeping his nails trimmed can help make this loving behavior more pleasant (see the section "Other Alternatives" later in this chapter for more on clipping nails).

Cats also use their claws for scratching not only the cat tree or your furniture, but for scratching themselves. There's nothing like a good scratch when something itches, and cat claws are perfect for this. Although cats generally use only the hind paws for scratching itches, they use their front paws for grooming, and this sometimes includes the claws.

The Mechanics of Claws

Other than the cheetah, all cats have retractable claws. This means that the cat can sheath her claws and extend them at will. Most cats have 18 claws all around: four on each back paw and four, plus a dewclaw, on each front paw.

A cat's claws are an extension of her skin, a complex part of the epidermal structure, and are attached to the terminal bone of the toes. The nerves and blood vessels that run through the claw form the pinkish line you can see running into the claw. This is called the quick.

The dead, white outer layer of tissue must be sloughed off regularly to expose the new growth underneath. If it is not removed, the nail continues to grow and can cause health problems. It interferes with

Something Extra

Polydactyl, a word that sounds more like a dinosaur than a cat, is the term used for cats that have extra "fingers." Many polydactyl cats have extended dewclaws that resemble a thumb, but the gene that produces polydactylism is often responsible for the cat having more than the usual number of claws, as well.

I have one polydactyl in my house, Candy, and she not only has the extended dewclaws on her front feet, but one extra claw, like a dewclaw, on one hind foot. So, instead of having 18 claws, she has 19. I have even seen polydactyls with six or seven claws on *each* foot, front and back. That's a lot of claws!

mobility, as the cat's claws get caught as she walks, and if allowed to grow too far, the claw can actually grow back into the pads of the paws. It's important to allow your cat to scratch as she needs to. Keeping the claws clipped also helps keep the nails in shape.

Scratching Problems

I have known several people who gave up their indoor cats or began allowing them outside because the cat was scratching their furniture, carpets, walls and other surfaces, and the owner was tired of the expense of replacing the items. In each of these cases, I asked the owners if they had a scratching post or cat tree in their house. The answer was always no.

What did these people expect? You can't assume a cat will simply give up an instinctive behavior just because her owner has not made the appropriate resource available. The cat will find her own resources—in other words, scratch whatever is available and appropriate to the cat.

You know that your cat needs to scratch, for many reasons. The trick now is to make sure your cat knows where *to* scratch and where *not* to. In other words, you must redirect your cat's natural needs from the inappropriate area to one you find suitable. To do this, you must first provide the cat with something on which to exercise her claws.

Cats need to scratch for their health and well-being. Providing your cat with appropriate places to scratch will help prevent damage to walls and furniture.

Cat Trees and Posts

Cat trees and posts come in almost as many shapes, sizes and colors as cats do. Finding a scratching post or tree to fit your home shouldn't be difficult. The key is finding ones that suit your cat's scratching tastes. Every cat is different and each has her own preference for scratching surfaces. Buying a cat tree or post your cat refuses to use (for whatever reason) is a useless exercise. You may as well not have one at all.

In our house we have several cat trees. In the living room there are two. One is huge with four tiers of curved perches and a tube that has three openings. The posts leading up to the tiers are made of different materials: two are natural wood and one is wrapped in sisal rope. The tiers, tube and base are carpeted. This type of tree is one of the best, because it allows the cat variety in which area she chooses to scratch. A few of our cats prefer to scratch natural wood—one cat in particular always used the wood trim on the walls until we replaced it with plastic trim and bought the scratching tree.

A variety of tiers and surfaces will make the cat tree more interesting than your furniture.

The other scratching post in the living room is all carpeted—just a plain post leading up to a box on the top that the cats like to sleep in. Other trees and posts around the house are of various sizes and are made of different materials. And all are used daily not only for scratching but for sleeping and playing as well.

When we first brought home the large tree in our living room, the cats went bonkers. They ran up it at breakneck speed, scratched every post and perch, attacked one another playfully and chased each other up and down it. With a cat on each perch, they would bat at each other from above and below. Of course, that initial enthusiasm has warn off somewhat, but the fact of the matter is that they have not touched the sofa since. And the tree is still used daily for play and sleep, as well as scratching and stretching.

When purchasing a cat tree or post for your cat, keep in mind your cat's particular desires, preferences and personality. Ask yourself several questions: Where does your cat like to scratch and what surfaces seem to be her favorites? Where does your cat spend most of her time and in what room does she do the most scratching?

In addition to these questions, base your buying decision on common sense and the innate behavior of all cats. As mentioned earlier, cats scratch for several reasons, and these reasons should be kept in mind when purchasing a tree or post for your cat(s) to scratch.

First, cats scratch to slough their claws, and for this they like a scratching surface they can really dig their claws into. Therefore, you need to purchase a tree with a surface your cat prefers. Some cats like to scratch the carpet. Carpeted posts are the most common and come in a variety of colors that can match your furniture.

Some cats like the rough surface of the *back* of carpeting, although I've never seen a tree or post made with the back side of the carpet facing out. To remedy this, you can make your own if you wish. Some people will stand a roll of carpet, back-side out, in a location where the cat will use it. I remember one time I bought carpeting for the house. I placed the roll in the kitchen leaning up against the dishwasher. The cats were all over it, scratching and using it as a makeshift bridge to climb up.

Sisal rope trees and posts, with their rough surface almost like that of the back side of carpet, can sometimes be an acceptable alternative. Tightly woven fabrics, hemp, bark and even corrugated cardboard are all good surfaces that a cat can dig into and not only remove the hulls from her claws, but also get in a good stretch.

Scratching is also a form of territory marking, your cat's way of saying, "This area is mine." This innate behavior is an important one to consider when determining where you will place the tree or post. Where your cat prefers to do her scratching should be where you place her scratching furniture. Most cats seem to prefer the living room furniture, but I have also known cats that like the walls, and even the kitchen table. To place the tree or post in one room when the cat does most of her scratching in another room is futile. She may use the post or tree on occasion, but she will also continue to use your sofa, or whatever other surface she prefers.

Cats love to look out the window. A tree with tiers for the cat to rest on, placed in front of a window, will ensure the tree's use. A window with a view of bird feeders will raise the chances of the tree being in almost constant use.

Last, and definitely not least, is the fact that cats stretch when they scratch. A cat will not use a tree or post that is going to tip over or move

Cat Post Criteria

+ Tall enough so the cat can stretch to full length
+ Made of a material the cat will enjoy scratching
+ Sturdy base
+ Un-tippable

whenever she digs her claws into it and pulls. Buy a tree or post with a good, solid base. The base should be larger in diameter than the top or the largest part of the main area of the tree or post. What I do is test the tree myself while it's still in the store. I tug at the top as if I were a cat climbing up it. If it tips easily, I move on to the next one.

It is also important to take into account the cat's size when fully stretched out. A post that is too short won't do the cat much good, since cats like to stretch to their full length when scratching. The average scratching post is usually too short for this.

Although most cat trees are more expensive than a simple post, they are also more widely preferred by cats, for obvious reasons. If you are worried about expense, weigh the price of one cat tree against the price of periodically replacing your sofa, and you will see that the benefits outweigh the cost. In the long run, you will save money and your cat will be happier.

In addition to cat trees and posts that are set on a base, there are also many types of scratching pads and hang-off-the-door scratching furniture available commercially. Some are impregnated with catnip to draw the cat to them. Most are made of corrugated cardboard (which some cats will scratch, others will ignore), and there are even carpeted pads available that you can attach to the wall. Some cats may be just fine with these, but often they are not enough. Either they are not stable enough and tend to tip or move, or they are not large enough for the cat to use to full advantage. If your cat will use these, great. But if they are all that's provided, often a cat will use them along with your sofa. Usually it's better, for you and the cat, to buy a good-quality scratching tree or post that meets all the cat's needs.

For all the reasons mentioned, scratching trees that are made of two or three different materials are best. Usually you can find posts that are made all of carpet, trees made from carpet, wood and rope, and a variety of other combinations. The more choices you give your cat, the better the chance that she will prefer her post or tree to your furniture.

With one cat, the tree you purchase may not have to be as elaborate as the one you will need if you have many cats, but the tree should still be tall, sturdy and effective.

I cannot stress enough the importance of a good, sturdy, tall cat tree! Chances are you can find one that is less expensive than declawing surgery would cost, and your cat will definitely prefer the tree. Simply put, if your sofa, chairs and other furniture are more fun to climb, scratch and run up and down than the tree or post you provide, your cat will use your sofa, chairs and other furniture! *Buy a tree your cat can have fun on.*

ONE POST OR TWO?

Recently, a friend of mine asked me why her cat was still using the sofa and other furniture to satisfy his urge to scratch, even though she had provided him with a scratching post. The first question I asked her was what *type* of post she provided for him. "Just a regular post," was her answer. "How tall is it? What is it made of? Is it the only post in the house?" After several questions, I discovered this post was not only too small for her cat, but it was the only area in the entire house she provided that was suitable for scratching. I recommended she spend the money to buy a tall tree made from different materials and place that in the cat's favorite area, and then put the post in another area of the house that the cat uses.

Too often, people think that all they have to do is buy one cheap, little post and their cat will automatically use it and leave everything else in the house alone. But generally the post ends up untouched and the furniture continues to be destroyed.

Cat Tree Criteria

+ Good, solid base (wider than biggest part of the tree itself)
+ Does not tip
+ Tall and steady
+ Preferably multi-tiered
+ Made of more than one material

Experts recommend, for good reason, that you provide more than one scratching area for your cat. Often cats will scratch in more than one place, and if you place a scratching pad, post or tree in each location you will lower the odds of your cat using your furniture.

In a multi-cat household, more than one scratching area is a necessity. Trees with multiple tiers provide a place to scratch, plus a place to sleep and play. As with any area of the house, a group of cats will establish territories. More than one scratching tree provides the cats with a variety of places to sleep and play, therefore lessening the chance that a fight will break out. Also, it will provide the cats with plenty of places to mark their territory.

You can buy different types of trees, posts and pads to place in various locations, but it's important to place them in areas that your cat(s) scratch. For one cat, a smaller but good-quality tree plus a smaller, stable post is usually sufficient (though, as with anything, there are exceptions). If your cat will use the cardboard pads and still likes to scratch many areas around the house, try placing a good-quality tree or post in her favorite spot, and the cardboard or smaller pads everywhere else. The more cats you have, the more posts and trees should be provided.

"But I've just obtained a new cat and don't know where or what she likes to scratch yet," you might say. In a case like this, your best bet is to purchase one or two trees or posts made with a variety of materials and place them in the most obvious locations—wherever there are surfaces a cat would like to scratch, such as the living room with its perfectly scratchable furniture. It helps to purchase several posts and trees and place them in various locations before the cat arrives. Then, you can always move them if you find your new cat scratching an area where there is no tree or post.

The More the Better

It's important to provide more than one place for your cat to scratch! You should provide two or more pieces of scratching furniture for your cat in her favorite places to scratch. And don't forget to *train* your cat that these are the appropriate places to scratch, at the same time distracting the cat from your furniture.

Scratch Post Training

Here comes the tricky part. You bought your tree and post and have placed them strategically around the house. *Now you must get your cat to use them!* I hardly had to train my cats at all once we bought the multi-tiered tree. It was so much more fun than the furniture that the cats preferred it. But there are still occasions when a cat will have to be chased away from the chair.

Placing the post or tree in an area your cat frequents is a start, but sometimes cats will scratch the tree and post as well as the furniture. You have to make sure your cat *knows* where it's appropriate to use her claws and where it is not allowed.

As I mentioned in Chapter Two on teaching a new cat the house rules, make sure when you bring a cat into the house that you show her from the start where her own furniture is. If you catch her scratching an inappropriate area, use a squirt bottle (remember, *no* hitting) to scare the cat away from that area. Or you can act as mamma cat by taking the cat gently by the scruff of the neck and shaking her lightly. Don't lift the cat off the ground and don't be too rough; simply give a little shake with a growl or verbal reprimand, then release the cat.

Immediately place the cat by the tree. Show her that this is the right place by scratching the post with your own nails and then taking the cat's paws and moving them up and down the post, much the way you train a kitten to use the litter box (see Chapter Four). Say "Good kitty," and praise the cat, even if she doesn't scratch or just looks at you as if you are nuts. If the cat uses the post, it's time for a celebration. Let your cat know she just did something great.

Play with your cat near her post or on her tree. Some cat trees or posts come with toys built into them—yarn and balls or springs with pom-poms on them that most cats love to bat at. Playing with your cat will give her a positive association with her tree or post and help draw her there even when you are not available to play.

Catnip rubbed on the post or a catnip spray can also help to attract the cat. But keep in mind that the effects of catnip only last for a short time and the catnip will eventually wear off. For this reason, it should be applied repeatedly during the cat's entire training, and even after as a reminder.

When you are not home to supervise, you may want to try confining your cat, if possible, to one room equipped with food, water, litter box

*Cat trees can also serve
as playhouses and
hideaways, making them
even more enticing to
your cats for scratching.
(Natalie Chapman)*

and scratching post. This way, you can be there to supervise when the cat has free run and does something wrong, or right. With a kitten, you can try the crate training explained in Chapter Two.

But confinement shouldn't be necessary except in severe cases. Most cats will find a really good cat tree made of carpet, wood and rope more fun and appealing than the furniture—particularly the tall, multi-tiered cat trees; I highly recommend those simply because cats love them. They can do so much more than just scratch them—more than they can do on a simple sofa.

BREAKING BAD HABITS

Okay, so you have a cat that is already accustomed to your sofa or other furniture as her scratching place. Now what? This is a little more complicated, but not impossible. At the same time that you are attracting your cat to the right place to scratch, you should be doing what you can to make inappropriate places unattractive.

Pet supply stores and catalogs often sell plastic covers that can be fitted over the sides of your sofa to protect the material. Any type of surface that a cat does not like to scratch can work. Sometimes placing double-sided tape or tin foil over the area the cat likes to scratch can deter her from that area. Just about any smooth surface that does not allow the cat to get a grip with her claws can be used to cover your cat's favorite (but inappropriate) scratching spot.

With a little ingenuity, you can set up safe "traps," an object that makes noise when the cat scratches, or something small that falls and frightens the cat away from that area. I've even heard of people who have fastened balloons to the sofa so that the sound of them popping frightens the cat away.

Of course, doing all this alone will not be enough, because soon your entire house will be covered from floor to ceiling with balloons, plastic and tin foil. Not a pretty picture! You will also have to set out several cat trees in various locations, and use a firm but gentle hand to train.

The type of furniture you have will also make a difference. Some materials are more scratchable than others. We have in our house a sofa with a plastic wicker-look frame. No fun to scratch, so the cats leave it alone. Tightly woven materials are the most fun and easiest to get a good grip with claws, so if you replace your furniture, keep this in mind.

Also, if it's feasible, try buying or replacing scratching trees when you replace furniture. Move the furniture around, placing the trees, posts and pads into areas that will help draw the cat away from the new furniture. For instance, place the best tree nearest to the sofa, a post near a chair, etc. This will give the cat an area of her own amidst her owners, and her own territory to mark. Plastic coverings on new furniture can be left in place until the cat is regularly using her post. Then it should be removed only when you are there to watch the cat and be sure she does not suddenly "discover" the new furniture. Eventually, when you are sure the cat will stick to her post or tree, you can leave the coverings off permanently.

The Perfect Deterrent

Not too long ago, I had in my home the perfect cat-scratching deterrent: my Doberman Pinscher, Dillinger. Although never specifically trained to do so, my dog learned through watching me tell my cats "No" whenever they scratched the furniture that scratching there was a no-no. For years Dillinger took it upon himself to stop the cats whenever they scratched the furniture. As soon as he heard them scratch, he'd run over and knock them away with his muzzle. Of course, once we got the cat tree, it took some time to teach the dog that it was okay for the cats to scratch there.

The Declawing Controversy

Should your cat be declawed? Declawing, simply stated, is the surgical removal of the claws, either on the front feet alone (which is the most common) or of the front and hind feet. Declawing (medically termed onychectomy) is an operation in which the cat is put under anesthesia and the claws, as well as the cells that promote claw growth, and the third phalanx (the last of the three toe bones) are removed. Afterwards, the area is sutured, and the cat goes home after an overnight stay in the hospital.

There is quite a controversy about whether declawing is mutilation, a form of cruelty, or not. Some say it is better to declaw than to get rid of a cat that insists on scratching up the house. There is a point here, but the effects of declawing on the cat should be considered carefully.

When trained properly, almost any cat will happily use a scratching post or tree. In most of the cases I have seen, the owners either gave up too soon, not wanting to take the time to train their cat, or they declawed the cat without trying at all.

But there have also been cases where everything possible was tried and the decision to declaw was weighed carefully: Declaw the cat, get rid of her or put her to sleep? The choice, in the end, was declawing, which saved the cat's life as well as the owner's sanity and expense.

But is declawing cruel? As with any controversial topic, some say yes, others say no. The reasons for these contrasting opinions are as varied as cats themselves. Despite some opinions and studies to the contrary, some cats have developed severe behavioral problems due to declawing. Kitty Angels Humane Society has seen many cats come to the shelter with behavioral problems that developed as a result of declawing. Autumn, a beautiful long-haired tortie female at the shelter, will never be re-adopted. Because of declawing surgery, she developed the habit of urinating everywhere except the litter box. She was fortunate her owners brought her to Kitty Angels, a no-kill shelter, rather than to the pound, where she would most likely have been euthanized.

One friend of mine, who had her first cat declawed, vowed ever thereafter never to do it again. She said her cat was in pain for weeks and refused to use the litter box, her feet became sensitive, and the cat was visibly stressed. Although the average time for recovery after declawing is three days, often it takes longer.

A cat that has been declawed *does* know that her claws are no longer there. Some declawed cats learn to resort to biting and using their teeth, since their ultimate defense weapon, their claws, is not there to assist them. When trying to stretch, a declawed cat cannot dig in and anchor herself, as a cat with claws can. Grooming and scratching are affected, as well.

Many veterinarians in Great Britain, and even some in the U.S., refuse to perform the operation, and it is illegal in some countries. Declawing is also seen as a no-no to most cat registries. Many no-kill cat shelters, such as Kitty Angels, have a strict no-declawing policy (as well as must-be-kept-indoors policy) for the cats they adopt out.

On the other hand, some cats do just fine and show very little, if any, effects from the procedure once their feet have healed. Kittens in particular adjust more easily than adult cats do. Some owners of declawed cats that have had no problems with the procedure claim that the surgery improved their attitude toward their cat. Since the cat was no longer clawing up the furniture, the owner was happier and the relationship between cat and owner improved.

Some apartment complexes fear destruction of their property and will be reluctant to rent to owners of cats with full claws intact.

Since there is no way of knowing beforehand whether or not your cat will be affected long term by this surgery, declawing should be done only as a last resort and only if absolutely necessary. Talk to your veterinarian before taking this step and, as with any big decision, think it through carefully.

Other Alternatives

Besides declawing, there are ways to stop a stubborn scratcher from damaging your property. One is keeping the cat's nails clipped. This will not stop your cat from scratching, but any damage will be greatly minimized.

The only problem with this is that most cats hate to have their paws held while their nails are clipped. Starting with a kitten is easier. If you get your cat accustomed to having her paws held at a young enough age, and work your way up to nail clipping, often the cat will learn to accept it and possibly even enjoy the attention.

Hold the cat's or kitten's paws gently and rub softly, allowing the cat to get used to the feeling. Never force the cat to hold her paws still. If she wants to go, let her go.

Talk softly and let your cat know that this is a great experience to be loved and enjoyed. Often, choosing a time when the cat is most relaxed, such as when she's in your lap, will create a more positive atmosphere for the cat to associate this experience with.

When your cat or kitten is comfortable with the paw holding, it's time to try clipping a few nails. Clippers made for cats work best. Expose the

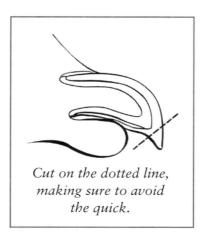

Cut on the dotted line, making sure to avoid the quick.

Nail Covers

Developed by Dr. Toby Wexler of Lafayette, Louisiana, Soft Paws are soft vinyl caps that fit over each nail, almost like false nails for a person. With the nails safely covered, the cat can still indulge in scratching behavior without damaging to the furniture. Soft Paws are available commercially, or you can ask your veterinarian for more information about them.

claw gently by holding the paw and putting light pressure on the top and bottom of the paw, just near the claw, until the claw is completely visible. Snip the end of the nail, being careful not to cut the quick (the pink vein inside the claw). It may take several tries over a couple of days to cut all the claws, because if your cat gets frightened it is best to stop and wait. Keep working with the cat and be positive about it.

This method has worked with most of my cats. All accept having their paws held, but a couple still refuse to have their claws clipped. The moment the clippers come into view, suddenly they forget that they love the attention of having their paws held. With these cats, often I must catch them while they are in a sound sleep and only do one or two nails at a time—as they generally wake after the first or second nail and catch on. Oh well, you can't win them all!

Flexor tendonectomy is another type of surgery that is less stressful and harsh than declawing. With this surgery, the tendons that are used for retracting the claws are cut, which makes it impossible for the cat to flex her claws. There is no overnight stay and cats recover more quickly with fewer negative effects than declawing. But, as with declawing, there are drawbacks to this type of surgery. Some cats still can't get a good stretch, and some cats don't recover as well as others.

Working with your cat to correct inappropriate behavior will bring the two of you closer, so long as you use plenty of love and patience. In the long run, the time spent getting to know your cat and the results of better behavior will ensure a closer relationship between the two of you.

Cat Hair Everywhere

All right, you have a cat. You're finding cat hair in your morning coffee, on your work clothes, in your bed. Basically, everywhere. Having an indoor cat, or more than one indoor cat, means more cat hair around the house than you would have with a cat that spends most or all of her time outdoors. But cat hair doesn't have to drive you crazy. In this chapter I'm going to discuss cat hair, helpful hints on keeping it in check, and also ways to clean up other little kitty messes that can occur with an indoor cat.

The Cat's Coat

In nature, a cat's coat is useful for many purposes, such as keeping the cat warm, protection from the elements and even camouflage. Generally, there are three types of hair that make up the cat's coat. For warmth, the cat has two layers of fur: the soft, thick *down* hairs, which are short and grow close to the skin; and the *awn* hairs, which are slightly longer and stiffer. The *guard* hairs, which form the top layer of fur, provide camouflage and protect the awn and down hairs from the elements.

On every cat, these layers are of varying lengths and thicknesses. All three layers on a longhaired cat are longer and thicker than they are on

111

a shorthaired cat, giving the coat a more plush feel. With the advent of breeding and domesticity came still more variation in coats and colors. There are not only cats with long hair and short hair, but now there are also cats with short, curly coats (Rex cats) and even almost bald cats, such as the Sphynx, which has very soft down hairs that are almost invisible.

Regardless of whether the coat is long or short, most cat breeds go through coat changes, particularly in the spring and fall, when one type of coat is shed away and another replaces it. In nature, and with cats that are frequently outdoors, these changes are more prevalent as the daylight time varies, not (as may seem the case) when the weather changes. But since indoor-only cats are constantly exposed to artificial light, most of them shed year-round.

Unfortunately, all this cat hair ends up everywhere—on your sofa, in your food, on your clothes, on the floor, on the drapes. The more cats you have, the more cat hair you have around the house. For allergy sufferers, this can be a problem (though it's the dander and not the actual hair that affects allergies).

And cat hair can not only be annoying, it can be damaging, too. More than once we have had the furnace repair man here to fix a problem that was largely due to cat hair clogging the motor. Electronic equipment can easily be ruined by cat hair. VCRs, televisions and computer drives can all get clogged with cat hair and can cost a lot of money to fix. Although you can't rid your home completely of hair, you can control it and keep it from damaging your property. There are several ways to do this, the first of which starts with your cat.

Grooming

Anyone who owns a cat has seen the process by which they groom themselves. Short, backward spikes on a cat's tongue allow them to clean the fur, pulling debris, parasites and loose hairs from their coat.

By pulling and rearranging the hairs during grooming, a cat is able to aid in the regulation of her body temperature. The grooming process also keeps the cat's coat healthy by stimulating the *sebum* glands, which are located at the base of each hair. These glands are responsible for the oils that lubricate and waterproof the fur.

Most cats do an excellent job of keeping themselves clean. Indoor cats tend to be much cleaner than their outdoor counterparts, simply

Cats can spend hours every day grooming themselves. (Beth Adelman)

because they are exposed to less dirt and they allow themselves more leisure time for grooming.

Since cats are so wonderful at keeping themselves groomed, you may be wondering why you should bother stepping in at all. But the fact of the matter is, there are reasons why you should help your cat in her grooming process. All cats, whether long hair, short or even bald, should be brushed or combed in one way or another on a regular basis. Of course, the longer the cat's coat, the more often this needs to be done, but every cat benefits from it, and so will you.

For one thing, look at all the hair that ends up in your brush when you groom the cat—this means there's that much less hair on the sofa and around the house. Also, the more you help your cat to rid herself of that loose fur, the less likely your cat will be to suffer from hairballs (those horrible little matted wads of fur that cats swallow when they groom, then later vomit onto your best carpet). That helps not only you,

Brushes can also be tasty and fun.

but the cat as well, as hairballs can sometimes cause blockages in a cat's intestines if they become too large.

Your cat's coat and how well the cat keeps it groomed can also tell you a lot about the health and well-being of your beloved pet. A dull coat, excessive shedding, bald patches or lesions can be a sign that something is really wrong and your cat needs to see the veterinarian.

Grooming your cat will also help strengthen the bond between cat and owner. Most cats, if properly introduced to it, will enjoy regular grooming, which will give your cat and you something to look forward to and share.

GROOMING THE LONGHAIRED CAT

Sammy has an unusually soft, thick undercoat that is plush and soft, and guard hairs that are long and beautiful. Everyone who touches him marvels at his clean, well-kept coat. But Sammy doesn't keep his fur this luxurious on his own, and the task for me is a constant one. Because of the thickness of his coat, it mats very easily, especially in the summer. Even my Himalayan, Mikai, does not mat up as easily as Sammy.

Since he was a kitten, I could see Sammy would have a gorgeous, yet difficult to maintain coat, so I began brushing him regularly right from the start. Now, when I take out his brush he comes running, rubbing against the brush and rolling around so I can brush him from top to bottom. This makes my job much easier, since I brush him at least twice a day and comb him out once every two or three days.

With any cat, grooming should begin at as early an age as possible to get the cat accustomed to the feel of the brush. Longhaired cats, in particular, will need a regular regime of brushing, so making this a positive experience for them will benefit not only the cat, but will make it easier on you as well. I use a slicker brush (the kind with a flat head and thin, bent pins) because the stiff bristles rake the fur, helping to prevent mats from forming.

Be gentle when brushing, no matter what type of brush you use. Don't tear at the fur, as this can be painful and give the cat a bad impression of brushing. When I was first getting Sammy accustomed to a daily routine of brushing, I would brush only the top part of the hair, gradually and gently working the brush deeper into his fur. He grew to love the attention, and your cat probably will, too.

As I mentioned with Sammy, longhaired cats should not only be brushed every day, but combed regularly as well. Although Sammy has no fleas, I use a flea comb on him every couple of days or so. I find that flea combs, with their closer teeth, are better at parting the hairs and preventing mats. As with brushing, be careful not to pull at the fur and cause your cat pain.

You'll need a slicker brush and a metal comb with close teeth to groom your longhaired cat.

Use a comb to get at the area on the head and around the face, avoiding the cat's eyes, ears and mouth (and don't get the comb caught on those whiskers). Work your way down the cat's back and tail, and be sure to get underneath as well. Mats tend to form most readily under the cat's arms, between her legs, on her belly and behind her ears, so pay special attention to those areas.

Sammy is unusual in that he does not mind me brushing his rear area and underneath him. Usually, he'll just roll over for me. When he's not in the mood to roll over, I lift Sammy's front legs up with one hand while combing or brushing underneath with my other hand. Usually a cat will only tolerate this for a very short period of time, however, so work carefully but quickly. Don't force your cat to remain there if she does not want to.

Brushing, although it helps remove many dead hairs, only loosens even more hair that the cat licks off or that falls to the floor. Don Kuehl of Manchester, Connecticut, owns a longhaired cat named Teri. He offered me this tip on how to keep loose hairs to a minimum after brushing. Don says, "After I brush Teri, I take a damp rag (not too wet) and rub her down with it. Terrycloth works best, as it catches most of the loose hairs that are left behind after brushing."

A couple of haircuts for longhaired cats, one called a lion clip and another called a kitten clip, can be done by groomers to keep shedding down and make brushing less of a duty (though still a necessity).

DEMATTING

There are times when mats just seem to form, regardless of your regular brushing. When this happens, the mat will be easier to remove the sooner you catch it.

Be careful not to pull at mats when you brush or comb your cat. If you come across a small mat, grasp it near the base, closest to the cat's skin. Starting at the top part of the mat farthest from the cat's skin, work the comb through the mat using sweeping motions. Make sure you keep a firm enough grasp on the base of the mat to prevent any pulling on the

Leave It to the Pros

If your longhaired cat develops mats that are large, numerous and/or close to the skin, you should let a professional groomer deal with it rather than trying to take care of it yourself. Often the cat will need to have the mats shaved off and the rest of the coat bathed to get rid of small mats and prevent further matting.

cat's skin that would hurt. Work your way up the mat slowly, until you have worked through the entire mat.

Pet supply stores sell de-tangling sprays that soften the mat and help the comb work through it. Talcum powder on the mat can help it comb out easier, as well. There are also combs that are specifically made to remove mats.

If a mat is too large or too tight to be combed out, you can clip it by using blunt-edged scissors. Be careful not to touch the skin when you clip. For mats that are too close or too numerous, a groomer or your vet can shave them for you.

GROOMING THE SHORTHAIRED CAT

Though it's not as vital as with longhaired cats, shorthairs need to be groomed as well. They also shed, get hair all over and develop hairballs.

For shorthairs, a soft-bristled brush is preferable to a slicker brush. After brushing, comb the cat to catch any hair the soft brush loosened. Follow with a nice run-over with a chamois cloth, and your shorthaired cat will remain slick and beautiful.

A bristle brush is fine for your shorthaired cat.

Bathing

Most indoor cats never need to be bathed. Unlike outdoor cats, indoor cats rarely get into anything dangerous or that they can't wash off on their own. But even so, there may be times when something will give you reason to help your cat with her bathing process.

Show cats are regularly bathed to keep their coats in top condition. Besides aiding in the health of the coat and control of shedding, bathing may be required if parasites are present and a flea bath is needed. Some smaller mats can be removed more easily if the cat is bathed and a dematting shampoo or conditioner is used. A case of excessive diarrhea can cause a longhaired cat to become messy and need to be bathed. If your cat gets a toxic substance on her fur, or gets into something so dirty that she cannot clean it off herself, she will require a bath as well.

But cats hate water, right? Well, for the most part, yes, cats hate being *immersed* in water. Gentleness and patience are key rules, particularly for a cat that reacts violently to being bathed.

Most show cats are bathed from a very young age, and although they may not grow to actually like it, most will learn to tolerate it. You don't have to have a show cat to begin bathing your cat at a young age. Remember, however, not to bathe too often, lest your cat develop dry skin. Once a month should be sufficient.

Before beginning the cat's bath, make sure everything is ready and within reach beside the sink or tub where the bathing will be done. Prepare the following items:

+ Soft bath towel (preferably terry cloth)
+ Washcloth
+ Shampoo specifically for cats
+ Tearless baby shampoo
+ A towel or mat for the bottom of the sink
+ Mineral oil
+ Cotton balls

Where you choose to bathe the cat depends on you. Many people prefer to bathe their cats in a sink equipped with a spray hose attachment. This is a good idea, as the nozzle can be held against the cat's skin, reducing the noise of running water, which frightens many cats. Other people like to "suffer" with their cat by running bath water in the tub and getting in with the cat. Also available commercially are small tubs made just for cats that hold the cat in place, enabling you to have both hands free to concentrate on bathing.

However you choose to do it, make sure it is most comfortable and calming for the cat. For the purpose of simplicity, I'm going explain a bath as given in a sink. You can modify the information for your own convenience and preferences.

Before beginning, place a mat or towel at the bottom of the sink. This will help keep your cat from slipping around, which could cause her more fear. Fill the sink with an inch or two of water and adjust the water temperature. You want the water to be warm, not too hot and not cold.

It is advisable to clip your cat's nails beforehand to help avoid painful scratches. Next, thoroughly brush the coat to remove loose hairs. Be gentle and calm. Place a few drops of mineral oil in the cat's eyes and cotton balls in her ears. This will help to keep out the shampoo. Some cats, however, will not tolerate this, and it will only make matters worse—don't force the issue. If this is the case, leave the oil and cotton balls behind, but be very careful when washing your cat's head.

If you can get an assistant to help hold your cat during the bath, great. If not, be careful, especially if your cat is not accustomed to baths. You may want to wear protective gloves.

Place your cat in the sink, holding her scruff with a firm grip and her back facing you. Wet the cat thoroughly with the nozzle of the hose or a container of warm water (don't push your cat under a running faucet), making sure you get all the way to the skin. Try to eliminate splashing sounds (that may frighten the cat more) by holding the nozzle or opening of the container gently against the cat's body. Do not spray the head or face, as this too can cause a panic. Use the washcloth to dab small amounts of water around the cat's face.

Once the cat is thoroughly soaked, take a handful of cat shampoo and run it through the coat, rubbing it in and creating a good lather. Don't forget to get the cat's belly and tail. Speak to your cat in a soothing tone to show her this is not a punishment, but is for her own good.

Place a tiny amount of no-tear baby shampoo on the washcloth and carefully wash the cat's face. Use just one finger rather than your whole hand, as this will make it easier to get around the eyes, ears and mouth.

When the cat is thoroughly washed, rinse with the spray nozzle as before. Rinse her face using the washcloth, as you did before. Never spray water in a cat's face. Once all traces of the shampoo are removed from the coat, you may use a conditioner made for cats if you wish. Rinse thoroughly.

When done, wrap your wet kitty in the terrycloth towel and keep her warm. Don't allow any drafts or chills to get to the cat.

After a good towel drying, comb the cat's fur carefully to prevent matting, particularly with longhairs. You may blow-dry the cat if she is willing, but be careful not to get the blow dryer too close to the skin and keep it on a low setting. Brush the fur backwards as well as forwards using a slicker brush as you blow-dry. Blow-drying is best done on longhaired cats to keep the coat fluffy.

Remember to hold your patience throughout the entire process to help keep your cat as calm as possible.

If your cat simply will not allow you to bathe her, no matter what method you use to restrain her or how calm you are about the whole thing, you can use a dry or self-rinsing shampoo. Ring 5 has a good self-rinsing shampoo called Quick Clean that is good for an on-the-spot cleaning.

A Healthy Coat

Keeping your cat in top condition will keep her coat healthy and prevent excessive shedding. Dr. Allan Levinthal, veterinarian at the Bolton Veterinary Hospital and Emergency Clinic in Bolton, Connecticut, says, "Shedding is a natural phenomenon but can be lessened if the skin is healthy. Excessive shedding is sometimes a sign of poor health in general or skin health in particular. Some individuals do have poorer skin health than others and do shed more. By correcting general health and skin conditions, these can be minimized."

Mineral oil in the cat's food will help combat dandruff and dry skin, which will, in turn, aid in preventing excessive shedding.

Did You Know?

Grooming is a form of self-protection for cats in the wild. Since wild cats eat live animals as prey, they get the blood on their fur, which could attract larger predators. Grooming removes this blood, keeping potential predators away.

Home Sweet Cat Home

Besides grooming, bathing, brushing and keeping your cat healthy, the way to minimize cat hair in your home is through general cleanliness and by using a few simple tricks that will make cleanup in your home simpler. This may sound like a lot of work, but it doesn't have to be. Ten or 15 minutes a day is all it takes to keep cat hair from carpeting your home.

Vacuuming may seem the obvious way to keep cat hair picked up, and in general it is. Although I use a canister-type vacuum cleaner with a beater bar, I have heard that the uprights work better at getting cat hair from carpets because they reach deeper into the pile. But canisters work as well, and the longer hose attachments make vacuuming in out-of-the-way areas easier.

Vacuuming should be done every day, particularly in multi-cat households, to keep cat hair to a minimum. But vacuuming the carpet alone won't get it all. As I learned, cat hair gets into everything, including furnaces and electronics. If your cat spends a good amount of time near your furnace, you might want to vacuum around it to keep cat hair away. I usually remove the door to the furnace and vacuum around the motor once a week. Also vacuum around your computer equipment, behind the refrigerator and around fans, air conditioners, televisions, VCRs and other electronics regularly.

Those little tumbleweeds of hair that blow by your feet and lodge in the radiator can be cleaned up during on-the-spot cleaning using a hand vac, if you have one.

Vacuuming alone can't get cat hair out of everything, however. Even though my cats are never in my car unless they are confined to a carrier, my car seats, being cloth, are still covered with a fuzzy layer. This is from the fur that sticks to my clothes, which is transferred to the cloth of the seats. To clean them, I generally run my hand along the layer of fur, rolling it into a ball and loosening it. I vacuum those hair balls, then use a lint brush to loosen and remove what is left. The same method can be used on sofas and chairs.

A strip of masking tape, sticky side out, can be wrapped around your hand to remove hair from clothes and even furniture. You can buy rolls of a sticky paper that is used the same way. A damp sponge wiped across your couch will also roll the hair into little balls that are easily removed.

As for furniture, cat owners often find that furnishings made from wood, metal, plastic and ceramics are the easiest to keep clean in a cat-filled home.

Sofa covers, washable cushion covers and chair covers are not only attractive, but will keep cat hair off your furniture, and they can simply be thrown in the washing machine. On the same note, towels and cat beds can be placed in the locations your cat prefers to sleep, which will be where the most cat hair will accumulate. Choosing furniture with patterns or in darker shades will make cat hair less noticeable. If you have one cat or even two cats of basically the same color, you can choose covers or even furniture to match the cat.

Houses with many cats obviously have more of a problem with cat hair than those with one or two cats. Hardwood floors coated with

The Light Shedders

If you want to avoid cat hair for the most part and still have a cat or two, there are several breeds of cats that shed very little. The curly-coated Cornish Rex has a coat of tight hair that sheds very little. The Sphynx, as I mentioned earlier, has almost no hair at all. But these cats need to be kept warm constantly.

The Bengal and the Singapura, although they have beautiful coats, I have heard are light shedders. If you are interested in any of these cats, I would advise visiting a cat show and speaking to breeders or ask your veterinarian if he or she knows of a breeder in your area who specializes in these cats.

polyurethane and area rugs are easier to keep clean in multi-cat households than is wall-to-wall carpeting.

Dusters that use a magnetic material to attract dust and debris are now available. Cat hair is also picked up by these dusters, and they are great for cleaning around valuables and in hard-to-reach areas.

Air filters not only keep the air fresh and clean, they can also help keep cat hair and dander down, which benefits allergy sufferers.

Other Cat Messes

Owning a cat means hair is not the only thing you'll have to clean up. Other little messes will invariably be left around the house from time to time, regardless of the breed of cat you choose. Those fur balls get coughed up onto your sofa or carpet, or the cat misses her litter box or chooses another area to relieve herself for whatever reason.

For a good way to remove a coughed up hairball or the product of a dinner eaten too fast, my cousin, Linda, says she picks up what she can with a paper towel, then she sprinkles baking soda on the area, leaving it there until it dries. Once hard and crumbly, the baking soda can be removed with a vacuum cleaner, hand vac or dustpan and broom. The baking soda soaks up any moisture that is left after the mess is picked up with a paper towel. A squirt of Resolve Carpet Cleaner and a slightly damp rag run over the area will take care of anything that may be left behind.

Litter box lapses can be cleaned using the same method with one variation. Since you don't want the cat returning to that spot, after blotting away the moisture with a paper towel, use an enzymatic cleaner that breaks down organic matter and pour it into the area. The baking soda can be sprinkled on afterwards, and when all is cleaned up, the lack of odor should prevent the cat from returning. Keep the area covered until it's dry. Try taping something that the cat finds unpleasant over the area: double-sided tape, tin foil or one of those office floor mats with the spiked side up. Besides cleaning the area, you can use a carpet deodorizer regularly when vacuuming to cover any surface odors.

Using a dust-free litter and locating the box on an easily cleanable surface will keep down tracking and dust in the air. For more information on litter box problems and solutions, see Chapter Four.

Safe Cleaners

Beware of cleaning your cat's eating or sleeping spots with chemicals that may be harmful to the cat, such as anything containing tar, coal, carbolic acid, wool tar or cresol.

Feed your cats on a mat using non-tippable dishes (ceramic bowls are good, or weighted stainless steel) and on a cleanable surface. Cat food cans should be rinsed out before being put in the recycle bin or thrown in the garbage so that they don't stink up the house.

Safety Outdoors

Cats love basking in the sunshine, sniffing the fresh air and watching butterflies. Just because your cat is indoors all the time does not mean she can't enjoy these pleasures. There are options available to the indoor-only cat owner who wants their cat to continue enjoying a romp in the sunshine.

Whatever option is right for you will depend on various factors such as the cat's personality, your finances and where you live. Certain situations (if you're renting your home, for example) may limit which options you can choose, but there are still always other options available.

Outdoor Enclosures

If you own your home or have permission to build on your property and have a little imagination and building skills, you can create an efficient and attractive outdoor enclosure for your cat(s). Even if you haven't the building skills or money to afford carpenters, you can still provide an outdoor enclosure for your cat's fun and safety.

The options are limitless when you set out to build your cat's enclosure. It can be a structure as simple as a small chain-link run or as elaborate as an entirely fenced yard. You can build an access door to the enclosure using a cat door or a window.

CHAIN-LINK

There are store-bought chain-link enclosures available for anyone looking for an easy and quick run for their cats. Sears sells eight-foot exercise pens, which are a good start for your cat's outdoor excursions. Make sure you buy (or build) a chain-link enclosure that is escape-proof. That means no gaps the cat can slip through and all sides enclosed, including the top.

A chain-link enclosure can include perches and extra additions, or you can build your own. Adding a tree, plants (nonpoisonous) and toys will help make this enclosure an ideal escape for your cat.

PORCH, PATIO OR BALCONY

Another simple yet effective idea is to screen in an already existing porch, patio or balcony. You might want to build runs, ramps or climbing trees in the screened area for your cat's amusement. I screened in my porch for my cats, and they love to sleep in the sun on the shelves I built within it.

But be *extra* careful to secure the screening around any balcony, especially on upper floors, to prevent falls. Even for agile cats, falls can be fatal.

Screened enclosures are a safe way for your cat to enjoy the outdoors.

Window perches can help bring the outdoors inside.

Window Perches

Window perches or boxes are inexpensive and simple ways for your cat to enjoy the fresh air and sunshine, although they do not provide the freedom to run. However, most cats will still enjoy just being able to lie in the sunshine and smell the fresh air.

Gardens

For the person with a green thumb and a love of cats, the two can be combined to make a cat-friendly solarium or indoor garden. This sounds like something only the wealthy would have, but a garden can be modified to fit almost any house or even apartment (if the landlord will allow it).

A garden or solarium can be almost any size and can be built on a screened or glassed porch, or in a sunny room of the house. A small garden can even be created on or near a windowsill.

Since this is for your cat's benefit, any exposed plants in the garden should be cat-friendly. Plants such as grasses, valerian, catmint, cat thyme, Japanese matatabi and catnip are examples of plants cats enjoy, and some can be dried to make homemade cat toys. If you choose to put flowering plants or others that you don't wish your cat to nibble on in the garden, chicken wire around them can keep them and your cat safe.

Since cats love to use dirt as a commode, you may want to use chicken wire or another device to keep the cats from digging in the garden. Or, you may want them naturally fertilizing your garden every day.

An outdoor cat enclosure, like the ones mentioned earlier, can also be turned into a kind of cat garden. Even a few plants or trees within it will give your cat a feel for the outdoors, plants to hide in, bugs to chase and sunshine to enjoy.

Other Ideas

If you wish to get more elaborate, many interesting ideas can become reality using simple chicken wire and wood. Tarps can be used to cover part of an enclosure for shade, ramps can be built for climbing and trees may be added.

Not too long ago, a friend showed me pictures of an outdoor enclosure a relative had built for her cats. It was constructed like a small house, screened in and done up in white painted wood. The shingled roof kept out rain. Within were not only shelves and ramps, but cat trees, a litter box and lots of places to play. A tube ran from a basement window into the enclosure so the cats could get to it from the house with ease, and the owners did not have to worry about rain or wind penetrating the opening.

A cat door is one way to make sure your cat can always get inside.

A fenced yard can also be made a safe haven for cats. The fence should have a small enough mesh so the cats cannot escape through it (stockade fencing is ideal) and be low enough to the ground (or built into it) so they cannot get under it. The fence should be at least six feet high, and chicken wire or metal can be placed horizontally over the top of the fence to prevent the cats from escaping over it. It can also be placed over tree tops to keep the cats from climbing the trees and getting over the fence.

There are disadvantages to outdoor enclosures, however, and you should be aware of these so they can be avoided. Make sure your cat always has access to the indoors whenever she wants. During inclement weather, your cat may not want to be exposed to the elements and will need to get inside, even if you are not available to let her in.

Also, a cat that goes outdoors is exposed to pests and parasites such as fleas, ticks, worms, snakes and dangerous insects. Keep any runs or enclosures flea sprayed with a vet-approved yard spray.

With a little care and caution, your indoor cat can enjoy a safe time and still reap the benefits of outdoor exercise.

Leash Training

Yes, cats can be trained to walk on a leash. They will not, however, heel by your side as a dog will. But with proper introductions, training and acclimation you can take your cat outside safely with you in control.

Before I explain the basic steps, there are a few warnings to leash training. First and foremost is to always use a harness specifically made for cats. *Never* use a collar, as it can slip from the cat's neck or may strangle her.

Harnesses for cats come in three basic styles: the figure-eight harness, the H harness and the V style. The figure-eight harness is one of the best for walks outside, since it tightens if the cat pulls, therefore preventing the cat from slipping out. There are also harnesses where the leash and harness are all one unit.

The leash should be of a lightweight material, not a big, bulky kind like you would buy for a dog. You can even get a leash and harness that match one another.

*A figure-eight harness is one of the best
for walking cats.*

One other caution to leash training is that many cats, once taught to go outside, will continue to want to go out, even if you are not in the mood for a walk. They learn quickly where the door is and may slip out unexpectedly—without the leash. Taking the cat out in a carrier (with harness on) or through a different door other than the one that is used for people may help prevent this.

Following are the basic steps for training your cat to walk on a leash. It is best to start when the cat is young, but an older cat can learn, too. It is also important to make sure the harness you use is of the proper size and is placed on the animal correctly. You should be able to slip two fingers between the cat and the harness when it is in place. To get a harness that fits your cat properly, take your cat with you when you purchase it, if you can.

Warning!

If you plan to tie your cat on a line outside, do not leave the animal alone. The cat will be vulnerable to other animals. Also, don't put the line near a tree that the cat can climb up and then get the leash or rope caught.

Step One

Familiarize the cat or kitten with the equipment. Place the harness and leash on the floor in front of your cat, allowing her to inspect them. Using the leash like a toy, play with the cat by dragging the leash along the floor like a string. Make the leash a fun item, something to enjoy.

Step Two

Once your cat or kitten has become familiar with the harness and leash, slip the harness on and buckle it, but do not hook the leash on yet. Let your cat get accustomed to the feel of the harness by itself.

Some cats will act as if you have just put some horrible restraining device on them and will roll around and try to get it off. If your cat acts this way, do not take the harness off. If you do, the cat will only learn that this behavior is rewarded by removal of the offending harness. Instead, distract the cat with play or a treat.

Do not leave the cat alone while she's in the harness. Keep watch until she begins to calm down. Once your cat has relaxed, take the harness off.

Step Three

Continue to place the harness on your cat every day, preferably several times, for longer and longer periods until your cat is completely accustomed to it. Tell the cat how good she is and give rewards for good behavior.

Step Four

Next, hook the leash to the harness. Hold the leash loosely and do not drag, pull or tug at it. Follow your cat around the house, wherever she wants to go. Don't expect your cat to walk at your side like a dog. However, you can help things along by offering food rewards as you walk slowly ahead, enticing the cat to follow.

Step Five

Once your cat is walking easily with you, it is time to take her outdoors. Be careful where you walk with your cat. It's best to stay away from highways or busy streets, or anywhere there may be aggressive animals or other dangers. Loud noises may frighten your cat, so take her to quiet spots to walk and relax.

Do not let your cat walk on neighbor's lawns or eat grass, because it may have been sprayed with insecticides or lawn chemicals.

Keep in mind that some cats are easier to train than others. Some will take to leash training easily, others may never get accustomed to it. Don't force your cat to walk with you, and never force a shy cat to go outdoors if she doesn't want to. Some cats just do not enjoy being outside—it frightens them. Other cats might become wild or uncontrollable. Some cats simply would rather stay in the house. For these cats, window sills or screened porches are a better alternative. Know your cat and her reactions, and have a good time in the sunshine with your friend.

CHAPTER EIGHT

The Healthy Cat

The first step in keeping your cat healthy is to know your cat. You should be in tune with your cat so that you will know when something is wrong. You will know something is not quite right by such signs as:

- ✦ Change in behavior
- ✦ Change in appetite
- ✦ Increased urination
- ✦ Vomiting
- ✦ Diarrhea
- ✦ Depression
- ✦ Lameness
- ✦ Stiff joints
- ✦ Increased thirst
- ✦ Coughing
- ✦ Sneezing
- ✦ Respiratory difficulties
- ✦ Runny eyes

These are just some of the changes that may be signs of an ill cat. Knowing your cat well will help you recognize other changes.

The Home Health Exam

An important part of knowing your cat is performing regular home health exams. These are not difficult to do and may help you to spot physiological changes you may otherwise have missed. These exams should be done during grooming sessions, and ideally started when your cat is young. (If you've acquired an older cat, please don't skip the exam. It just may take a little time to accustom the cat to the handling.)

When beginning your exam, start by looking at your cat overall. Is her behavior normal? Is she standing and walking properly? Does the cat's balance seem correct? Any noticeable changes should be immediately brought to the attention of your veterinarian.

For the physical exam, you may want to use food treats, and don't forget the praise. Keep your cat calm throughout the exam. If at any time the cat begins to get agitated, it is best to stop and continue at another time when she is more relaxed. Negative associations will only make future exams more difficult, for you as well as the cat.

Start your exam with the cat's eyes. They should be bright, clear and free of excessive discharge. A small amount of clear discharge may be normal, but thick, dark discharge may be the sign of a problem, such as a blocked tear duct or conjunctivitis, and should be brought to the attention of your veterinarian.

If your cat bumps into things or seems to have trouble deciphering distances, you will want your veterinarian to check her eyesight. When I acquired Teisha, I noticed her movements were slow and cautious. If an object was on the floor that had not been there previously, she would walk into or trip over it. Her pupils dilated normally, but a trip to the veterinarian indicated a retinal detachment that caused her blindness.

Check the lenses of your pet's eyes. Do they seem normal? Cloudiness may be a sign of cataracts. Redness or discharge around the lids may mean conjunctivitis.

Next, look into the cat's ears. They should be clean and pink, but not red or swollen. A foul odor is the sign of an ear infection. If the ears look dirty, or if the cat scratches at them continually, ear mites may be present.

Check in the cat's mouth. Most cats resist this, and you will need to be easy and gentle. Place your hand over the cat's head and, using your thumb and middle finger, press lightly on either side of the cat's mouth until it is opened. The gums should be pink, not white, bluish or yellow.

Lifting one lip carefully, press on the gums. They should turn white at your touch, then quickly return to their natural color. There should be no foul odor from the mouth. This can mean an infection or even kidney or digestive problems. The teeth should be white, not yellow or brown.

Brushing your cat's teeth using a pet toothpaste (ask your veterinarian) or a baking soda and water mixture is a good idea. Do not use any toothpaste made for humans, as they may make a cat ill.

It's okay if your cat's nose is dry, but there should be no excessive nasal discharge.

Now, feel your way down the cat's body. Start at the neck and throat, feeling for any lumps or sore spots. Check for fat. If you can't feel your pet's ribs, it may be time for a diet. On the other hand, if the ribs are sticking out or are more prominent than normal, the cat is losing weight. This could be the indication of a serious health problem.

Next, gently pull up the skin on your cat's neck. The skin should fall right back into place when released. If the skin remains, your pet may be dehydrated.

Looking through your cat's coat, check for fleas or other parasites. Flea dirt resembles tiny specks of pepper and turns red when dampened.

Become familiar with your cat's normal pulse rate. Check it for any changes whenever you do her health check. You can feel the pulse by gently pressing right behind the cat's left front leg over the chest area. A normal heart rate should run between 110 to 240 beats per minute.

Respiration should be even and barely audible (unless, of course, the cat is purring). Open-mouth breathing, holding the head extended while breathing or excessive chest movement is abnormal and should be checked by a veterinarian.

Next, run your hand down the cat's legs and paws, and feel for any abnormalities (such as swelling, pain, lumps or stiffness). Also, watch your cat when she walks. Being familiar with her normal gait will help you spot a problem, such as a limp, in advance.

Finally, look around your cat's anal area for excessive redness or discharge. If she has tapeworms, they may be visible and resemble small bits of rice. However, it is still a good practice to have your cat's stool checked for internal parasites whenever she visits the veterinarian.

Cats have anal sacs located on either side of the anus. Occasionally, anal sacs get impacted and may cause irritation. If your cat is scooting her hind end along the floor or licking excessively at her anal area, have a veterinarian check her for impaction.

The entire exam sounds like a lot of work, but once you and your cat become accustomed to the routine of a home health exam it should not take much time at all, and will benefit you both in the long run.

Neutering Your Cat

I have spoken to people who think that because they are not letting their cats outside where the animal can breed freely, they don't have to have the cat neutered (spayed or castrated). Some people cringe at the very idea, as if they will be harming the animal or denying it some fun. But the truth of the matter is that a cat's sexual "desire" is merely instinctual. Cats do not mate for pleasure.

A cat that is not neutered and is kept strictly indoors will drive you crazy trying to get out. Females caterwaul all night when in heat, and males (and even some females) spray foul-smelling urine to mark territories and to attract a mate. The fact that they are indoors will not change any of these instinctual behaviors. Instead, your cat will be frustrated that he or she cannot fulfill his or her biological drives.

A cat that is "fixed" is also healthier. Intact cats have a higher incidence of testicular (males) and ovarian (females) cancer.

Rumors of cats becoming fat and lazy after neutering are false. As long as you adjust the cat's food intake to meet the slower metabolism and continue with plenty of interaction and play, the cat will remain trim and healthy, and the incessant need to get out of the house to find a mate will diminish.

Besides all this, cats that are fixed are more settled and less antsy than cats left intact. So, do your feline friend a favor and have him or her neutered, if possible before sexual maturity sets in (at five or six months of age).

A neutered cat need not become fat, as long as she stays active. (Beth Adelman)

Vaccinations

A big controversy with indoor cats is whether or not they need annual vaccinations. Some claim that if an indoor cat lives in a high-rise apartment or other area where there is no chance of escape and no possibility of other animals coming into the home, then why vaccinate?

There are several reasons why indoor cats should be vaccinated, regardless of living arrangements. The immune system of a cat that is never exposed to any disease is weakened. Therefore, if the cat does become exposed the chances are higher that she will develop that disease and lower that she will recover. Vaccinating allows the cat to be safely exposed to certain viruses, strengthening the immune system not only for the disease the vaccination protects against, but also in general.

Also, you can carry germs and bacteria in on your own clothes. Veterinarian Dr. Allan Levinthal states, "Even though indoor cats may not have direct contact with other disease-carrying felines, you may!" Some contagious diseases can be transmitted through contact with inanimate objects, such as clothing, luggage, garbage and food. When these things then come into contact with your cat, she is exposed to the disease.

If you have other animals in the house that are coming in and out (such as a dog), there is a chance they could carry viruses or bacteria in with them, even if they have immunity. Rabies is a big threat in some parts of the country, and feline leukemia virus is one of the largest cat killers today.

The law is another good incentive for vaccinating. In Connecticut, where I live, the law states that all cats must be up-to-date on their

> ### *Recommended Vaccination Schedule*
>
> 1. Panleukopenia, Calicivirus, Rhinotracheitis at four weeks of age. *(Optional—recommended for catteries.)*
>
> **For Full Adult Immunity**
>
> 2. Panleukopenia, Calicivirus, Rhinotracheitis at eight to 10 weeks.
> 3. Panleukopenia, Calicivirus, Rhinotracheitis–Rabies–Feline Leukemia Virus at 12 to 14 weeks.
> 4. Panleukopenia, Calicivirus, Rhinotracheitis–Feline Leukemia Virus at 16 to 18 weeks.
>
> *Note:* Boosters are necessary every year to keep immunity at its proper levels.

rabies vaccinations. It does not matter if the cat is indoors or outdoors, lives in an apartment or a house. Connecticut is not the only state to have this law, so check the law in your area to be sure.

However, the vaccines for an indoor cat do not necessarily need to be as extensive as those for an outdoor cat, unless there is an indoor-outdoor cat in the household that can bring diseases in. (If there is, all the cats in the home should be vaccinated fully.) For example, annual feline leukemia virus vaccines may not be necessary for an indoor cat with no way out and no exposure to cats that go outdoors. Discuss all the options with your veterinarian.

Common Ailments

Although indoor cats are generally healthier than outdoor cats, like humans, cats do get sick once in awhile. The following is a basic list of some of the more common health problems that can affect your cat.

COUGHING

Should your cat develop a cough, she should be taken to the veterinarian to determine the cause. The most common reason for coughing is hairballs.

Never give your cat a human cough medicine, as they may contain chemicals that can do more harm than good. Your veterinarian can recommend the best medicine for the problem.

DIARRHEA

Diarrhea can have a variety of causes, from intestinal parasites or food intolerance to serious liver or kidney disease. Two safe and often-recommended medicines to use for a mild case are Kaopectate or Immodium A-D. Consult your veterinarian for the proper dosage.

However, if the diarrhea is severe, lasts for more than a few days or is accompanied by blood or mucus, take the cat to your veterinarian immediately.

HAIRBALLS

Hairballs (balls of hair that are ingested during grooming, then later vomited) can be a problem for all cats, but plague longhaired cats most frequently. If your cat is vomiting a lot of hairballs, a commercial hairball medicine such as Petromalt can help.

Make sure the hairballs come up and that your cat is eating, drinking and defecating properly. A hairball can cause severe problems if it gets caught in a cat's intestines. See your veterinarian for more severe cases, or if the cat is vomiting more than just hair.

ALLERGIES

Allergies can afflict cats as well as humans. Allergic cats will display many different symptoms, depending on the cat and the allergen.

Flea allergy dermatitis is one of the most common allergies seen in cats. Signs of this allergy include excessive scratching, biting, hair loss (particularly on the back and stomach) and red pimple-like lesions. The chemicals in flea collars can also cause an allergic reaction. If your cat loses the hair and develops redness under her flea collar, remove the collar immediately.

Cats can also be allergic to certain particles in the air such as pollens from plants, house dust and other inhalants. These kinds of allergies may be inherited. Signs include paw licking, sneezing, redness and scratching. The signs are about the same as those of flea allergy dermatitis, but no fleas are present.

Tests may be done through your veterinarian to determine the cause of the allergy. Cortisone injections are usually given to treat an allergy.

Cats may also develop allergies towards certain foods. If you notice a certain brand of food is causing itchy skin on your cat, cut that food out of your cat's diet and try something else.

Many cats have what is called food intolerance and will develop a loose stool with flecks of blood. Intestinal parasites must be ruled out, and then a diet should be recommended by your veterinarian.

Some cats develop an allergic chin rash or lip ulcer in reaction to plastic feeding bowls. Many veterinarians recommend crockery or china.

Intestinal Parasites

Although indoor cats are less likely to get internal parasites, they still can. Intestinal parasites are spread primarily by fecal-oral contact (ingesting eggs or larvae in some way, such as by licking another cat's anal area), and if you bring a new cat into the home, you could unknowingly be bringing parasites in with her. Some intestinal parasites can be obtained from killing and eating rodents (roundworms) or by ingesting insects (tapeworms), and even indoor cats can, on occasion, get hold of these pests.

Keeping your environment clean and using good sanitary practices with the litter boxes will help eliminate parasitic infections.

All intestinal parasites are diagnosed primarily through stool samples checked by your veterinarian. These checks should be done regularly, whether your cat seems sick or not, because there is a period of time after the cat is infected (the *prepatent period*) when she won't show clinical signs. This is due to the fact that it can take several weeks before eggs show up in the stool sample.

Commercial, over-the-counter dewormers are not recommended. Let your veterinarian choose the specific medicine that's best for treating your cat.

Following are some of the parasites that may cause problems for your pet.

ROUNDWORMS

Roundworms, one of the most common intestinal parasites to plague kittens and cats, are contracted primarily either prenatally (in the uterus) or by eating rodents. Signs of roundworms in kittens include thinness

> ### A Healthcare Tip
>
> Have any new cats tested for worms and disease before bringing them into your home, especially if you have other cats. If need be, keep the new cats in isolation until the results of all the tests are back, and until they have been dewormed.

with a pot belly, dull coat, vomiting, coughing and diarrhea. Adult cats can show no signs, yet still be infected with the parasite.

Roundworms are spaghetti-like worms that may be vomited by the cat in the case of a severe infestation. Two or more treatments may be necessary to kill all the parasites in your cat's system.

TAPEWORMS

Tapeworms are contracted primarily by ingesting infected insects, such as fleas, or may be spread by eating rodents or raw meat. The dried segments of the worms (and sometimes the live ones) can be seen on the anal area of the cat, and they resemble grains of rice. Other signs of tapeworms include weight loss and occasional diarrhea.

Keeping your cat free of fleas and making sure she does not eat rodents will help prevent tapeworms.

HOOKWORMS

Hookworms generally infect cats when the cat swallows them or their eggs. They may also penetrate a cat's skin or be contracted prenatally. Indoor cats have an advantage if you keep their environment clean. Make sure all potted plants or indoor gardens use sterilized potting soil.

Symptoms of hookworm infestation include diarrhea (often bloody), anemia and weakness. Two or more treatments may be necessary to rid kitty of these dangerous parasites.

COCCIDIA

Coccidia is an intestinal infection caused by a protozoa, and is commonly found in kittens. Adult cats tend to build up an immunity to coccidia.

Coccidia produces bloody diarrhea that may or may not be tinged with mucus. Medication is usually sulfa drugs, and good sanitation is important. It is also necessary to sterilize the environment after a coccidia infestation has been cleared.

HEARTWORMS

When people think of heartworms, they usually think of dogs, but, although rare, heartworms can infect cats as well.

Transmitted by the pesky mosquito, it's rare for indoor cats to become infected by heartworms, unless an infected mosquito gets into the house and bites the cat.

Heartworm larvae migrate through the animal's body and grow to maturity in the chambers of the heart. Signs of heartworm infection include weight loss, coughing, anemia, swollen abdomen and legs, vomiting, heart and liver damage followed by eventual death. However, if caught in time, injections of thiacetarsamide will kill the adult worms in the heart. As long as all goes well, another dose will be administered two months later to kill the microfilaria left behind in the animal's bloodstream.

If you are concerned about heartworm in your cat, a blood test, followed by preventive treatment, can help put you at ease.

External Parasites

As with internal parasites, external parasites such as fleas, ticks, mites and ringworm can plague our indoor friends. Knowing what to look for, what to do and how to prevent infestations will keep these little buggers in check.

FLEAS

At one time, battling fleas was one of the toughest challenges a cat owner faced. But today there are flea preventives that work unbelievably well and are safe for your cats and the environment.

Fleas can cause many problems for cats, including dermatitis, tapeworms and, in extreme cases, anemic reactions that may even lead to death. Small kittens, especially, should be kept flea-free. Heavy flea infestations have been known to cause high mortality rates in catteries, especially in the case of newborn kittens.

The best defense against fleas is prevention. These pesky little bloodsuckers love to breed and hide in carpeting, upholstery, cracks in wood floors and along walls, using your beloved companion (and you) as a hop-on meal.

Three of the most recent and, in my opinion, best flea preventives are Program, Frontline and Advantage.

Program, a tablet or liquid you give to your cat, works by interfering with the flea's breeding process. Thus, the number of fleas gradually diminishes, provided there are no animals coming in and out of the house carrying new fleas (and possibly pregnant ones) in with them. If your only pets are indoor cats with no exposure to other animals that may bring fleas into the house, Program is a fantastic method. At only a small cost per month, it is definitely less expensive than exterminators, flea bombs and dips, much less traumatic for the cat, and much safer for the environment.

Advantage is a liquid that comes in a small vial. The liquid is placed on the back of the cat's neck and kills any fleas that come into contact with the cat. I personally use Advantage and can vouch for its effectiveness. I have not seen a flea since we began using it on all our indoor animals.

Frontline is applied similarly, and comes in a vial, like Advantage, or in a spray. I would recommend the vial over the spray for cats, however, because sprays usually scare cats. Frontline works on both fleas and ticks. Frontline needs to be applied monthly for fleas or once every three months for ticks. Though it's rare for indoor cats to get ticks, they can be brought in on you or on another animal. For this reason, we use Frontline for our dogs, which all go outside, and Advantage for the cats and ferrets.

Whichever product you choose will depend on your preference, budget, number of cats and whether or not you have animals that go in and out of the house. Discuss these products with your veterinarian, as they are all available only by prescription.

These products can be expensive if you have many cats, but if you have trouble with fleas and are spending a small fortune on flea bombs, dips, exterminators and the like, they are well worth it in the long run.

Though they are easier and more efficient, you don't have to use any of these products to keep fleas in check. If you live in a place where fleas are not a big problem, you can keep up on the flea problem by vacuuming every day, especially in the warmer months. But be aware that fleas may breed inside the vacuum bag and reappear. You can try placing a flea-killing product, such as flea powder or a flea collar, inside the bag and vacuuming thoroughly (don't forget those cracks and crevices). If this is done routinely before the fleas appear, it can help keep their numbers to a minimum.

Some people mix brewer's yeast in the cat's food every day to keep fleas away. I'm not sure if this works or not. Some swear by it, others say it doesn't work at all. You can always try it and see for yourself.

Then there are always flea bombs, dips, sprays and powders if you want to go that route. When buying flea control products, ask your veterinarian for the safest and most effective brands to use on your cat. Pyrethrin dips and shampoos seem to be the safest and most highly recommended.

For flea collars, many people buy the chemical brands, while others prefer natural or herbal collars. If you decide to use a flea collar, make sure it is the proper size, and never put a flea collar on your cat after dipping, spraying or powdering. Combining insecticides can be lethal.

TICKS

Ticks can transmit many diseases to your cat and to you, including Lyme disease and Rocky Mountain spotted fever. If you find a tick on your cat, remove it immediately using a pair of tweezers. Grasp the tick near its head and pull out firmly and carefully. It may take a few seconds to remove the tick. Be sure you haven't left the tick's head embedded in the cat's skin, as this can cause a serious infection.

After the tick is removed, a lump may appear in that spot. This is normal, but watch the area for redness or irritation.

Check your cat for ticks when doing your home health exam. Pay special attention to ear flaps, head, neck, shoulders and feet. Ticks vary greatly in size, depending on the species and how long they have been on your cat. The most common ticks range from small, flat bugs (the size of the nail on your little finger) to approximately one inch around when they are engorged. The ticks that carry Lyme disease are very tiny and are barely visible without magnification, even when engorged, so do check carefully.

Safe Disposal

Dispose of a tick very carefully. *Never* crush them between your fingers, as that exposes you to any disease they carry. The best method is to put them in a jar with a little alcohol, and then seal the jar tightly.

RINGWORM

Despite its name, ringworm is not a parasite but a fungal infection of the skin that is highly contagious among cats and to humans. Circular, hairless lesions with a red outer edge, flaky skin and hair that pulls out easily are all signs of ringworm.

Ringworm organisms last in the environment for a long time. Cats will eventually clear the organism on their own (in weeks or months), but will serve as carriers to people and other pets. The treatment is an oral medicine prescribed by your veterinarian (Fulvicin) or a lime-sulfur dip and antifungal ointment.

For lesions on humans (circular or semicircular itchy areas, generally on the forearms and neck), an over-the-counter antifungal cream such as Tinactin should get rid of the problem in a few days.

Once you rid your cat of ringworm, discard or sterilize all cat-related items such as brushes, combs, leashes and bedding, as reinfection can occur.

MITES

Ear mites are the most common mites found in cats, and indoor cats are also prone to them (although not to the extent that an outdoor cat is). To check your cat for ear mites, look into her ears with a flashlight. Dirty-looking ears, scratching at her ears, tilting her head and keeping her ears in a horizontal position can all be signs the cat may have ear mites.

Your veterinarian can give you prescription drops to put in the cat's ears and instruct you on how to administer the medicine and how often.

Besides ear mites, there are also white mites, chiggers, maggots and lice. White mites resemble large particles of dandruff and can cause extreme itching. Flea sprays may be effective in helping to eliminate these, but in severe cases see your veterinarian.

A small orange or red mite attached to your pet's belly, ears, head or legs may be a chigger. If you remove one of these pests from your cat, watch the area closely for infection. For heavy infestations, ask your veterinarian for the proper insecticide.

LICE

Sometimes lice are hard to spot, as they are very tiny. Severe itching may be a sign that these microscopic pests are present. Lice are rare on cats, but can occur. Your veterinarian can make the proper diagnosis and give you a shampoo that will eliminate them.

Administering Medicine

Sometimes when cats get sick, you'll need to administer medicines at home. This can be a harrowing experience for both you and the cat if you do not know how. The first step in avoiding disaster is to ask your veterinarian to show you how to properly administer the medication, and pay close attention to how it is done.

When you are ready to give medication to your cat, it is best to have someone help you to restrain her. If this is not possible, wrap the cat in a large towel from the neck down. Make sure the towel is tight enough so the cat can't get her front legs up and through, but not so tight that you choke her.

Hold the cat with one hand, and administer the medicine with the other. You can place the cat on a counter or on your lap—whichever is easiest on you and calmer for the cat. I prefer to set my cats in my lap while at the same time holding the cat's legs between my own.

TABLETS

The most common medication you may have to administer at one time or another in your cat's life is a pill. Every cat reacts differently to taking a pill. Some pills have a flavor that cats find appetizing. If this is the case, the cat may eat them on her own with no help from you. But most pills just taste like medicine, and, for obvious reasons, most cats despise having their mouth forced open and a pill shoved down their throat. In these situations, good restraint and quick action are important.

Hold the cat against your body or have an assistant hold her for you. Place your hand over the cat's head, palm down, enclosing the head.

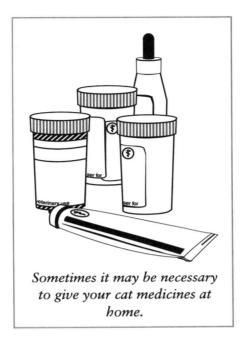

Sometimes it may be necessary to give your cat medicines at home.

Gently place your thumb and forefinger on the back corner of each side of the cat's mouth.

Tilt the cat's head back carefully and apply gentle pressure to the sides of her mouth. With your other hand holding the pill, gently push down on the cat's jaw and open her mouth.

Place the pill at the back of the cat's tongue as far as you can. Then gently place your hand around the cat's mouth while you close it, to prevent her from spitting out the pill. Stroke her throat to aid in swallowing. You can also blow a small, quick puff of air at the cat's nostrils—this stimulates a swallowing reflex. Slowly release your hand from her mouth. If the cat licks her lips, the pill has been swallowed.

Watch your cat carefully when you release her, just in case she's managed to fool you by hiding the pill deep in her mouth. If she has, she'll quickly spit it out, and you can try again. Feeding your cat a small treat while she's still in your lap may help to ensure that she swallows her medicine.

Some pills can be crushed up and hidden in the cat's food (get your veterinarian's okay on this before doing it), but usually if a pill is placed in whole, the food will be devoured and only the pill will remain. If you're giving medication this way, you must supervise while the cat eats to make sure all the medication is given and no other animals get it.

LIQUIDS

Liquid medicines can be given several ways. Some can be mixed with food, others can be administered with an eye dropper or syringe (without the needle). Ask your veterinarian which is best for the type of medicine prescribed and the exact dosage to administer.

If you're using a dropper or syringe, place one hand over the cat's head. With your forefinger, lift the side of the cat's cheek. Carefully insert the syringe or dropper into the cat's mouth and dispense the liquid slowly, giving the cat time to swallow.

Be sure to rinse the syringe or dropper after each use.

INJECTIONS

Injections are rarely necessary at home, but there are conditions, such as diabetes, where they will be required. If you must give injections to your cat at home, make sure your veterinarian shows you the proper method of doing it. If you have any questions or problems, don't hesitate to call your veterinarian and ask him or her what you need to know.

Make sure you keep all the equipment clean, and don't leave needles around on the counter for your cat(s) to find.

SKIN CREAMS AND OINTMENTS

Administering creams and ointments for skin conditions may be necessary to treat cuts, bites or abscesses, or to avoid infection around sutures. It is important to follow your veterinarian's recommended schedule when applying these, and to be sure the cat does not lick them off. Your veterinarian may recommend what's known as an Elizabethan collar—a large, round piece of material that fits around the cat's neck and prevents her from licking her body or scratching her head.

These collars are certainly not comfortable for a cat, so be gentle and patient if your cat needs one, and give her lots of extra love.

EYE OINTMENTS AND DROPS

To administer any eye medication, start by washing your hands. Then gently hold the cat's head still with one hand. Your forefinger should be just above the eye and your thumb below. Pull the eye open very gently, but not too forcefully.

With your other hand, squeeze the prescribed amount of ointment into the eye, being careful not to touch the tip of the tube to the cat's eye.

Close the cat's eye and hold for only a few seconds, allowing the ointment to penetrate the eye.

For eye drops, carefully wipe off the area around the cat's eye with a clean swab. Hold the cat's head as for ointment, and apply the prescribed number of drops in each eye. Then gently hold the cat's eye closed for a couple of seconds.

EAR DROPS

Hold the cat's head firmly, gently grasping the outer ear. Fold the outer ear back carefully and apply the drops directly into the ear canal, (*do not* stick anything down into the ear canal, as this can do damage). Then gently massage the base of the ear.

These are just some of the medicines your veterinarian may prescribe, depending upon the nature of your cat's injury or illness. Make sure you follow his or her instructions carefully, and don't hesitate to ask questions. Getting it right is vital to your cat's health and well-being.

Household Emergencies

Emergencies can and do happen, and it is a good idea to know what to do to ensure minimal suffering and maximum recovery for your cat, just in case. Even if no physical injuries are apparent, it's a smart idea to get your cat to a vet as soon as possible after an emergency, such as a fall. Internal injuries are invisible, and can prove fatal.

Here are some signs to watch out for:

+ Shock
+ Cold ears
+ Hot, sweaty foot pads or ears
+ Different-size pupils
+ Pupils not responding to light

+ Fever
+ Respiratory distress
+ Seizures

Even something as minor as a small cut should be looked at by a veterinarian, lest an infection set in.

PREPARATION

Emergencies, by definition, come upon you all at once. The first thing you need to do is remain calm. You will not help the cat or yourself by panicking.

It's much easier to keep your cool if you've done some preparation in advance. Here's what you can do:

+ Have a veterinarian who knows your cat. This way, any allergies to medicines or other health conditions will already be on record when the cat arrives at the hospital.
+ Keep a list of emergency numbers near your phone, including your regular veterinarian and an emergency animal clinic, in case your regular veterinary hospital does not have emergency hours.
+ Keep an emergency first-aid kit on hand for your cats.

In an emergency, do what you can to stabilize the cat, and then seek professional help. Look carefully at the cat and the situation, so you can figure out what has happened. By evaluating the cat and knowing what is wrong, you can help your veterinarian determine the best way to help your cat recover.

APPROACH

If the cat is conscious, approach her carefully. Cats can lash out in fear when they are injured, no matter how friendly they are normally. Move slowly and do not rush forward. Bend down to the cat's level slowly and speak in a soothing tone. Reach your hand slowly toward the cat. If she shows no sign of aggression, get her to the veterinarian as soon as possible, talking and reassuring her all the way (see the section "Moving an Injured Cat" later in this chapter).

Emergency First-Aid Kit

- Blunt-edged scissors
- Blunt-edged tweezers
- Tick remover (tweezers can be used, but commercial removers are available through your vet or pet supply shop)
- Gauze bandages
- Cotton balls
- Hydrogen peroxide
- Rectal thermometer
- Milk of Magnesia*
- Petroleum jelly
- Immodium A-D*

* Use these items only under the advice and direction of a veterinarian.

If, however, the cat lashes out at you, you will have to take steps to restrain her. A blanket, pillow case, towel or piece of clothing placed over the cat's head (allow room for breathing) is your best bet. Hold the animal firmly by the back of her neck.

Check for vital signs, particularly if the cat is unconscious. First, check to see if she is breathing. Check her heart rate if you can, and control any bleeding (see the sections "Bandaging" and "Tourniquet"). An injured cat may be difficult to work with, so get help if you can.

CHECKING PULSE, RESPIRATION AND TEMPERATURE

To check your cat's pulse, press your forefinger and middle finger against the inside of her inner thigh, near the groin. You can count the beats for 60 seconds or count for 15 seconds and multiply by four. The heart rate should be approximately 160 to 240 beats per minute.

Watch your cat as she breathes, and count either the inhalations or exhalations, but not both. Again, count for 60 seconds or 15 seconds and multiply by four. In a healthy cat, the respiration should be 20 to 30 breaths per minute.

To take her temperature, have someone hold the cat, if possible, or wrap the animal in a towel or other restraint that allows for free breathing. Using a rectal thermometer (the human kind is fine) lubricated with petroleum jelly, insert the thermometer into the cat's anus. Use gentle pressure until the thermometer is inserted about one inch.

Hold the thermometer gently in place for two minutes. The temperature should be 100.4 to 102.5 degrees Fahrenheit.

MOVING AN INJURED CAT

Be careful when moving an injured cat, whether she's unconscious or not. Injuries can be aggravated in transport.

Move an unconscious cat carefully away from any dangerous area using a coat or blanket supported underneath the cat. If you can get help, have someone else hold one end of the coat or blanket, or have them restrain the cat during the move. Be careful the cat does not slip from the blanket or coat. If a box or other secure container is available, gently place the cat inside for ease of transport.

If the cat is conscious and struggling, be careful. An injured cat may lash out. Speak in soothing tones and move slowly. Wrap the cat in a blanket or towel, making sure her paws are restrained but being careful not to aggravate any wounds. You can hold the scruff of the neck and support the legs to help subdue her. The cat should be placed in a carrier or box that closes securely and transported to a veterinarian immediately.

ARTIFICIAL RESPIRATION

For a cat that has stopped breathing but still has a heartbeat, start artificial respiration. Place the cat on her side, and open her mouth to check for any obstructions in the throat. Clean the cat's mouth of any blood or mucus.

With the cat's mouth closed, place your entire mouth over her muzzle and exhale *gently* until you see her chest expand. Remove your mouth

Caution!

Never practice artificial respiration or heart massage on a healthy cat. You could injure her.

from the cat's until you see her chest deflate. Continue this while transporting to the veterinarian or until the cat is breathing on her own.

CPR

CPR (cardiopulmonary resuscitation) is required if the cat is not breathing and has no pulse. This is a life-threatening situation, and CPR should be done immediately and continuously. For CPR to be effective, you must combine artificial respiration with heart massage. CPR will not be effective, however, if there is extensive external or internal bleeding.

Place the cat on her right side. Clear away any blood or mucus in her mouth and begin artificial respiration, as described in the previous section.

But you must also simultaneously perform heart massage. There are two ways this can be done. One method is to place your entire hand around the cat's chest so that her breastbone is resting in the palm of your hand. Your thumb and forefingers should be in the middle of the cat's chest. Another method, particularly if you have small hands or the cat is large, is to place the heel of one hand on the left side of the cat's chest, just behind the elbow. Place your other hand on top of that hand.

With either method, compress the chest for a count of two and release for a count of one. Continue this with the artificial respiration while transporting the cat to the veterinarian or until the cat's heartbeat is regular and she is breathing on her own.

SHOCK

After an injury, a cat may exhibit signs of shock: pale or white gums, rapid heartbeat, rapid breathing, confusion, low temperature. Check the cat's airway to be sure she is breathing normally. Check for and remove any foreign substances blocking the airway. Check for a heartbeat (perform CPR if necessary) and control any bleeding.

Keep the cat warm with a blanket or coat and roll up a towel or piece of clothing and place it beneath her hindquarters to keep them elevated. As with all emergencies, transport immediately to the veterinarian.

ELECTRICAL SHOCK

The first step is to get the cat away from the source of the shock. *Do not* touch an electrical cord or a cat that is being shocked; unplug the cord or move it away from the cat with a wooden object, such as a broom handle. Then feel behind the left front elbow for a heartbeat and check for breathing.

If the cat is breathing, transport her to a veterinarian immediately. If the cat is not breathing but there is a heartbeat, perform artificial respiration and transport to a veterinarian (simultaneously, if possible).

If the cat is not breathing and there is no heartbeat, perform CPR as you transport the cat to the veterinarian (if possible).

POISONS

Poisons can enter a cat's body more ways than simply by being swallowed. Some poisons enter through the skin or through open wounds. Others can enter the lungs through inhalation. Signs of poisoning vary but may include vomiting, convulsions, coughing, abdominal pain, diarrhea and delirium.

If your cat comes into contact with a poisonous substance, seek veterinary help as soon as possible. If you know what the poison was, take a sample with you and, if your cat is vomiting, take a sample of that, too.

With some swallowed poisons, inducing vomiting using hydrogen peroxide (one teaspoon every 10 minutes), followed by a few teaspoons of activated charcoal (available through your veterinarian), can help. Get the cat to the veterinarian as soon as possible.

However, if the poison is a petroleum-based compound or a strong acid or alkali, *do not* attempt to induce vomiting. Your poison control center can give you more information on the recommended action to take.

WOUNDS

If your cat gets a small wound, carefully clip the hairs around the area with a blunt-edged scissors, and wash the wound with soap and water. Then apply either hydrogen peroxide or Betadine to kill bacteria. Do this at least three times a day, making sure the wound stays free of dirt and foreign particles. Look for any signs of swelling or redness, which suggest an infection.

If the wound is extensive or bleeding can't be stopped, sutures may be necessary and veterinary care is required. A rash or skin infection should be treated by a veterinarian, as oral antibiotics may be needed.

Bandaging

Bandaging a wound may help keep the bleeding under control until you get to the veterinarian. To bandage a limb or tail, wrap gauze firmly (but not too tightly) over the wound. Next, place a strip of adhesive tape at the end of the bandage. Then wrap the tape securely over the bandage in overlapping bands. Bandage the entire limb and be sure the tape overlaps some hairs, to avoid slipping.

When bandaging a wound on the body, chest or abdomen, first place a piece of clean gauze over the wound. Take a large rectangular piece of cloth and cut one-inch strips on either side, about a third of the way into each side. Place the cloth so the uncut part fits securely around the cat's belly. Tie the strips over the cat's back. Transport the cat to the veterinarian immediately.

Tourniquet

If the cat is bleeding and direct pressure does not stop it, applying a tourniquet may help. Do not place a tourniquet over a joint or fracture. Any strip of cloth can be used as a tourniquet. However, do not use rope, wire or string.

Place the cloth about one to two inches above the wound. Tie a loose loop around the limb. Lay a strong stick or a sturdy pencil over the tie, and tie another loop on top of it. Twist the stick until the bleeding has ceased (no tighter). You will need to periodically release the tourniquet and then re-twist it as you quickly transport the cat to a veterinarian.

Splint

In the case of a break or fracture, applying a splint will help keep the bones immobile until you are able to get kitty to a veterinarian. The splint should be a long, rigid, flat piece of material. If the cat is in extreme pain or fights when you try to apply the splint, stop, wrap the break in a sturdy towel and transport her to a veterinarian immediately.

If the cat does not fight, place the splint over the fractured area, making sure the joints directly above and below the break are included. Tape or tie the splint securely, but not too tightly. You don't want to cut off the circulation. Transport the cat to a veterinarian immediately.

CONVULSIONS AND SEIZURES

Be patient. Most seizures seldom last more than a few minutes and are rarely life-threatening. Don't restrain the cat. Leave her alone unless she is in danger of hurting herself. Clear away any objects the cat could bump into or hurt herself on.

When the seizure has ended, the cat may be disoriented for 10 or 15 minutes. Calm her with affection and speak in soothing tones. Lower the lights and keep the house quiet. As soon as you've calmed your cat, call your veterinarian.

For a seizure accompanied by a high temperature (over 104 degrees Fahrenheit), place ice packs around the cat's inner thighs and under her front legs. If a seizure lasts longer than five minutes, or if the cat goes in and out of seizures for several hours, take the cat to your veterinarian. An injection of Phenobarbital or Valium may be necessary to stop the seizures, or a more severe problem may be present.

OBJECT IN THE EYE

Flush the eye with clean water or saline immediately. If a chemical was splashed into the eye, wrap a clean gauze pad around the eye to cover and protect it. If there is bleeding, apply pressure to the area until the bleeding has subsided, then wrap the eye. Transport the cat to the veterinarian.

BURNS

For second- or third-degree burns, place cold packs on the area of the burn and transport the cat to the veterinarian immediately. *Do not* apply ointments.

For mild burns, place ice packs on the affected area. Leave in place for at least 15 minutes. Cover the area with clean gauze, and watch it carefully for signs of infection.

SMOKE INHALATION

Remove the cat to an area where there is plenty of fresh air. Check the cat's breathing. Use artificial respiration or CPR if needed, treat for shock and seek veterinary care as soon as possible. Carbon monoxide poisoning should be treated in the same manner.

CHOKING

Signs include pawing at the mouth, pale tongue, distress and unconsciousness. Clear the cat's airway by placing your hand over the cat's head and gently pushing your thumb and forefinger on either side of the cat's mouth just behind the long canine teeth. Tilt the cat's head back carefully. If you can see the object, try to remove it with your fingers or tweezers. *Do not* attempt to remove a needle or other sharp object. Take the cat to the veterinarian immediately.

If you cannot remove the object, lay the cat on her side and place your palms behind the last rib on both sides of the abdomen. Press your palms together in a thrusting motion several times, firmly but carefully. If the object still does not dislodge, transport the cat to the veterinarian immediately.

If your cat has swallowed a string or thread and it is hanging from the animal's mouth or anus, pull gently to remove it. However, *do not* pull if you meet with any resistance. Transport the cat to the veterinarian.

To the Vet

None of the advice in the preceding section is intended as a cure-all. It is only as a way of stabilizing the cat to optimize her chances of survival. *Always* transport an injured cat to a licensed veterinarian as soon as possible.

Caring for a Sick Cat

If your cat is injured or ill but is able to come home, she will require special care and a lot of love from you. Being home in familiar surroundings will help speed your cat's recovery. So will your care and attention.

A sick cat should be placed in a separate room away from noise, household traffic and other animals. A bed should be made that is warm, soft, clean and washable. You can use a lined cardboard box or the cat's regular bed. A litter pan and food and water dishes should be set up near the cat's bed for easy access. Your veterinarian can recommend the best foods and feeding schedules.

Keep your sick cat warm and dry at all times. Remove any soiled bedding immediately and replace it with fresh bedding. Keep any medications your cat will require nearby, and be sure you know the proper methods and doses your cat will need. Never give your cat aspirin or any other type of human medication for any reason, as these may be toxic. Consult your veterinarian before giving any medications.

You know your cat best. However, follow your veterinarian's advice on any health or emergency situation.

Natural Disasters

In February 1986, a flood-weakened dam threatened to destroy Marysville, California. Many people were evacuated from their homes with little notice. In October 1990, fire swept through southern California, destroying homes and killing many humans and animals. On August 23, 1992, Hurricane Andrew devastated parts of Dade County, Florida. More than 100,000 cats and dogs were left homeless. In March 1993, a blizzard struck the Northeast and left behind lost lives and homes without power. On January 17, 1994, at 4:30 a.m., a major earthquake shook sleepers from their beds in southern California.

Regardless of where you live, a natural disaster is a real threat to you and your pets. Whether your area is susceptible to a tornado, hurricane, blizzard, earthquake, fire, flood or mud slide, you should not only prepare yourself, but also know how to protect your cats.

BEFORE DISASTER STRIKES

Prepare yourself. The Red Cross provides a pamphlet on disaster preparedness that offers information on what you can do for yourself in case of an emergency. Follow their advice on storing food, blankets, water, flashlights and medical supplies. After you've prepared a disaster kit for yourself and know what you will need to do, you can then prepare a disaster kit for your cat(s).

The following steps will help you prepare for a disaster. Then, if the worst should happen, at least you'll be ready.

Your Cat's Disaster Kit

+ Medical supplies, such as gauze, ointments and bandages
+ Special medications, if your cat takes them
+ Newspapers and towels
+ Leash and harness (one set for each cat)
+ Clear photographs and descriptions of each cat
+ Non-spill food and water dishes
+ Litter pan and litter
+ Plastic bags
+ Enough cat carriers or cages to hold all your cats
+ A week's supply of water and dry cat food

1. Devise a plan before disaster strikes so you will know what to do and be organized in the event of a quick evacuation. Your cat should be trained to enter a cat carrier without fuss (see Chapter Two).

2. Know your cat's favorite sleeping and hiding spots. If you are warned of an impending disaster and need to evacuate, you will not want to waste precious moments searching for the cat(s).

3. Keep your cat's vaccinations up to date. In a stressful situation, a cat's immune system is lowered. And if the cat is brought to a shelter, she may come into contact with bacteria that could cause disease.

4. Know in advance where you can go with your pet(s). Most evacuation shelters are for humans only and will not allow you to bring your cats with you. During a natural disaster, humane societies and animal shelters are usually overburdened, so finding alternate arrangements is essential. Maybe a friend in another area can help. If you are lucky enough to find a shelter that will allow you to keep your cat(s) with you, be sure you have an ample supply of food, water, litter and cleaning supplies. Do not remove your cat(s) from the carrier

> ## Save My Cat
>
> Some people place bright-colored stickers on their doors or windows that state how many and what types of animals are in the house. But, my brother, who is First Lieutenant of our local fire department, told me that emergency personnel don't always go by these because many people do not update the stickers and the firefighters cannot risk their lives trying to find an animal that is no longer in the house.

while in the shelter unless it is essential, and always use a secure harness and leash and do not allow cats to roam.

5. If you must leave your cat(s) behind, make sure they have an ample supply of dry food and water in non-spill dishes. Set the cat(s) up in a room away from windows or breakable objects. Keep cats, dogs and other pets separated, if possible. Fights can occur in traumatic situations, even among animals that are friends. Cats should have access to someplace high in the event of a flood.

6. In some disasters, such as with earthquakes, there will be no warning or time to evacuate. Having carriers and food supplies ready and knowing where to find your cat(s) can prevent problems. Make sure your cats are always wearing identification, preferably with your phone number and the number of an out-of-state friend. If your cat gets out of the house and becomes lost, you will want a number on the animal's tag that can be reached in the event your phones are out for days at a time.

THE AFTERMATH

Once the disaster is over, many cats will be extremely frightened and hide for days or weeks. Aftershocks from earthquakes can last for a long time and may cause some cats to continue hiding. It is essential that you keep the cat calm as best as you can. Pet, talk to and reassure the cat often, but do not force her from her haven (unless it is a dangerous area). Make sure the cat has food, water and a litter box available.

If you come home after an evacuation and find your home damaged or destroyed, arrange to have your cat(s) stay with a friend or relative until you are resettled. If you are fortunate enough to have your home spared from disaster, do what you can, if possible, to help others who were not quite so fortunate. Organize a neighborhood search for missing pets, or offer to volunteer at your local shelter or humane society. Teach public awareness on what to do before and after a disaster. Help others to keep their pets as safe as you want your cats to be.

C H A P T E R   N I N E

Where Did Kitty Go?

Even indoor-only cats can get out. A door inadvertently left open too long or a ripped screen can provide access for a curious cat's escape. An indoor cat that gets out, particularly a cat that has never been outdoors, could easily get lost, because she is not as familiar with the terrain as an outdoor cat.

With prevention and care you will spend many long and happy years with your companion and not have the worry and pain of a lost cat. However, there are steps you can take if this happens to your cat to help ensure the cat's safe return.

What To Do

Step one: Don't panic. Stop and think: How long has the cat been missing? Where, knowing your cat, would she go? Are there wooded areas the cat may have gone into, or a busy street nearby? Check with neighbors to see if they may have seen your cat. Walk the streets and woods calling for your cat. Get the help of others, if possible.

When Taffy disappeared, I formed a posse of friends and we searched the woods behind my house, which is where Taffy was last seen heading (a neighbor had remembered seeing her because she "had never seen that cat in the neighborhood before").

Use something that makes a sound your cat is familiar with and comes to, such as a can opener or squeaky toy. This may or may not help, depending on the cat, but it won't hurt to try.

If there is an abandoned building in the area, you might want to look there, or ask the police to look around (don't roam around inside abandoned buildings by yourself, as they might by dangerous). Check trees, parks, restaurants, garbage dumps and construction sites. Leave your name and phone number with everyone you come in contact with.

Photo ID

Always keep a good-quality, clear photograph of your cat available in case you should need it.

Step two: Call the police to report your cat missing. In larger communities the police will probably tell you to contact an animal shelter, and you should do this as well. Also contact pounds, pet shops and veterinary hospitals. Leave your name, phone number and a description of your cat with them.

Step three: If your cat is gone for more than a day, keep in contact with animal shelters, police, fire departments, pet supply shops and veterinarians. You will also want to make up posters at this point. Make one poster and copy it. You will want to distribute the posters around, so make plenty—100 or 200 posters. Many office supply stores or quick print shops can print up that many copies quickly and inexpensively.

Place the posters everywhere the cat may have gone, as well as all around neighboring towns and as far as you can in a radius around your area. Place them on telephone poles, in grooming salons, store windows, colleges or universities, schools, pet supply shops, veterinary hospitals, shelters or pounds and police and fire stations. Give copies to everyone you come into contact with, including the letter carrier, newspaper carriers and delivery persons.

Lost Cat

Your poster should have the following information:

- LOST CAT and REWARD should be printed in large, dark letters at the top. People tend to be more helpful if there is a monetary reward involved. However, you should omit the amount of the reward, to prevent extortion.
- A sharp, clear photograph of the cat should be placed in the middle.
- A detailed description of the cat—breed, color, size and any distinguishing markings—should be put under the photo. Put these in words that even someone unfamiliar with cats will understand.
- Your phone number(s) should be dark and legible and placed at the bottom of the poster. The phone number of a friend who agrees to be a contact can also be helpful.

Don't put your cat's name on the poster, or any sentence like "Answers to the name of . . ." (most cats in a strange situation will not respond to their name, anyway). Also, don't put on the poster clues about the cat's behavior, where it was lost (the cat may have been picked up and dropped off somewhere far away), its gender (someone unfamiliar with cats may not know the difference between a female and a neutered male), or whether or not it was wearing a collar (the collar may have slipped off or been removed).

If your cat is missing for more than a few days, change the posters regularly, just in case they are torn off or rained on.

Step four: Place an ad in the "Lost and Found" section of local newspapers, particularly daily papers. Also, check the ads for "Found Cats." Someone may have found your cat and put an ad in themselves. Call radio and television stations that offer advertising or public announcements. The more people you reach, the better.

Step five: If there is one in your area and you can afford it, you might want to hire a pet detective to help search for your missing cat.

Step six: Don't give up until you believe you have done all you can to locate your cat. Remember, there have been cases of cats that have disappeared for weeks or months, even years, then came home on their own or were found. If by some unfortunate fate your cat never returns to you, know that at least you did all you could.

Preventing Escapes

The first step in preventing escapes is to teach your cats that the door is off-limits. Chapter Two explains how to accomplish this.

The following techniques can either prevent your cat from getting lost in the first place or will help ensure a safe return should she manage to get out.

SECURE THE HOUSE

Check screens regularly, including those on doors, to make sure they are not torn and fit tightly. Make sure doors close properly. My cat Taffy got out because the screen door stuck open when it wasn't pushed closed.

*Make sure all your windows and any open doors are
securely screened to prevent escapes.*

INFORM GUESTS

Tell anyone who comes into your home that you have indoor cats, and ask them to close doors properly upon entering and exiting, and to be sure screens are placed securely in all open windows.

Identification

Keeping identification on your cat will prevent someone from thinking she is a stray and keeping her, or may help the cat be returned to you if she is found.

There are essentially three forms of ID available for cats. The collar and tag is the most common form of identification. A collar and tag with your name and phone number (address optional) can be kept on your cat at all times, if you choose, even though the cat lives indoors. Medical information and the fact that your cat is an indoor pet should also be placed on the tag.

Many types of tags are available, including metal ones or inexpensive, plastic reflective tags. They can be purchased easily at any pet supply store.

The collar should be expandable, so if it gets caught on something the cat can pull it off and will not be strangled. The collar should fit on your cat just loose enough that you can slip two fingers beneath it. Do not put tags on a flea collar, as they are not constructed for this purpose.

Tags come in all shapes and sizes.

That Clinking Sound

You may wish to keep only one tag on your cat's collar. Cats have very sensitive hearing, and more than one tag constantly clinking together can drive a cat nuts.

Acclimate your cat to wearing a collar when she is young, if possible. Some cats, if not accustomed to a collar, may practically kill themselves trying to get one off. They may get a paw or their jaw caught in the collar, and this can have serious consequences.

The disadvantage of collars and tags is that they may fall off or can easily be removed. They can also pose safety problems. If you live in a situation where your indoor cat cannot possibly escape, a collar is probably not necessary.

Another form of identification is tattoos. These can be placed on the inner thigh or inside the cat's ear. Most people opt to place the tattoo on the inside of the ear, because a tattoo on the inner thigh is not noticeable unless the area is kept shaved. The exception, however, is with show cats. Many cat registries forbid show cats to have a tattoo inside the ear. In that case, the tattoo should be placed on the cat's inner thigh.

The number you use for the tattoo is your choice, the most common being your social security number, a number chosen number by the tattoo registry or the cat's registration number (in the case of pedigreed cats). Whatever number you choose, it must be registered with a national tattoo registry, or even if your cat's tattoo is discovered, the finder will have no way of contacting you.

Usually a collar and tag with the tattoo registry phone number is also worn to alert people to the presence of a tattoo. But if the cat loses her collar and the tattoo is on the inner thigh and not shaved or readily noticeable, the shelter or pound picking up the cat may not know to look for a tattoo.

Tattoos are a reliable form of identification. However, they can fade with time and may have to be redone. Tattooing can be done by your veterinarian, breeders, groomers or at a tattoo clinic. Often towns or clubs will hold a tattoo clinic for people who wish to have their pets tattooed. For more information, contact Tattoo-A-Pet at (800) 828-8667 or I.D. Pet at (800) 243-9147.

Collar Safety

I recently witnessed a terrible tragedy, part of which was due to the use of a collar. A cat in my neighborhood, apparently lost for a long time (possibly an indoor cat that had escaped and lost its way), was attacked by a dog. In the bustle of getting the cat to the vet, I did not notice that she was wearing a brown, unbreakable flea collar that was snaked around her neck and down under one front leg.

Unfortunately, the cat did not survive the attack, and the reason for her inability to escape became obvious when the vet and I saw the collar. The area around the collar was raw, bald and festered. That cat had been suffering a long time.

Expandable collars, too, can sometimes get caught around a cat's legs or in her mouth. I've seen cats with cut lips and broken jaws from collars caught in their mouths. Break-away collars are a bit better, but it is vital with any collar to make sure it fits properly so that the cat cannot get a paw or her jaw up under the collar. Unfortunately, flea collars generally don't have tight enough buckles to maintain the right fit and will sometimes expand after lengthy use.

In my opinion, tattoos and microchips are far better identification than a collar. If you must use a collar on your cat, err on the side of caution and check the fit carefully and regularly. Do not leave flea collars on for more than a month, and always use the safest collar available.

The newest method in pet identification is the microchip implant. This is a tiny computer chip, about the size of a grain of rice, with a registered number. It is injected into the cat, usually between the shoulder blades. This is a permanent form of ID that cannot be lost or altered.

The disadvantage of this method, however, is it requires the use of a special scanning device to read the chip, and not all facilities own this type of equipment. Also, the chip technology has not yet been standard-ized, so facilities that have scanning equipment may not have the right kind to scan your pet's chip. There are several different types of chips and scanners available now, and not every scanner can read every type of chip.

But microchips are the wave of the future, and some communities that require cats to be registered are now giving the owner the choice of a microchip implant for their cats.

For more information about microchips, you can contact AVID at (800) 336-2843 or Infopet Information Systems at (612) 890-2080. Both run national registries for their microchips. The American Kennel Club also operates a microchip registration and recovery service that is open to all types of pets. You can call AKC Companion Animal Recovery at (800) 252-7894.

CHAPTER TEN

Cats in the Kitchen

For maximum health, your indoor cat will require a high-quality diet. A 100-percent nutritionally complete diet of the proper food can help prevent such problems as obesity, nutritional deficiencies, finicky eating and plant chewing, and will help your cat maintain a healthy coat and stronger immunity to illness.

Cats enjoy a variety of foods, including vegetables. Feeding your cat greens such as lettuce is fine, and even healthful, but remember that cats are true carnivores. Only meat provides the amino acid taurine, plus other essential nutrients cats need in order to survive.

You should choose a diet high in protein for your cat, with the proper amount of fats, vitamins, minerals and carbohydrates. Any cat food that states on the label that it is 100 percent nutritionally complete should be fine, unless your cat requires a specialized diet for a medical problem. The nutritional claim should say that the food was tested in accordance with procedures established by AAFCO—the Association of American Feed Control Officials, an association that sets the nutritional and testing standards for all animal feeds.

Cats should be fed a varied diet and not strictly fish, lean meat or liver, as these products alone will not be completely balanced and can cause deficiencies. Commercial cat foods offer many different flavors, and you can feed your cat any and all she chooses, as long as the cat does not have an allergy to a certain type of food or flavor.

For maximum nutrients and liquids, cats can be fed a combination of dry and canned cat foods. A kitten eight weeks to four months of age should eat three to four meals a day of a high-quality kitten food (canned and/or dry). As your cat gets older, her meals can be cut to two per day (starting at about one year of age).

How much you feed your cat at each meal will depend on the cat and the type of food you feed. Several factors should be considered:

+ Is your cat overweight?
+ Does your cat require a special diet? (If so, follow your veterinarian's recommendation.)
+ Are you feeding a high-calorie food?
+ Does your cat pick little bits all day long or gorge herself at every meal?

Dry food can be left out for your cats as long as they do not overeat or are not on a special diet. Also, it should not be allowed to spoil or get stale if the cat does not eat it. I leave dry food out for my cats, and the turnover is so quick that it does not have a chance to get stale.

My cats eat only what they want and do not gorge themselves. However, this is not true for all cats. If your cats eat more than the recommended amount, I would advise feeding two square meals a day and removing any leftovers.

My cats are funny—some of them hate canned food, and some love both canned and dry. So, I feed a quarter can of moist cat food (six-ounce cans) to each cat that likes it twice a day, and leave the dry food down for those that want it. To some of my cats the dry food is more of a snack than a meal.

My only cat with a weight problem is Teisha, my blind cat. I feed her only one-quarter can of food twice per day. On occasion, I will give her a handful of dry food as a treat.

It's a good idea to monitor your cat's weight as she grows. If the weight remains the same, continue to feed what you are feeding. However, if the cat seems to gain or lose weight, you can feed more or less until the cat's weight is steady.

Feeding Time

If you have more than one cat and they get specific meals during the day, they should be able to enjoy their meals quietly and without hassle. Feed each cat in a separate food dish away from traffic and noise. Some of my cats eat quickly and search out food from the slower cat's dishes. To prevent this, watch the cats as they eat to make sure the slower cats are allowed to finish their food. Feeding slower eaters in a different room can also be helpful.

Your cats can share feeding time, as long as they don't steal food from one another.

Cats should also be fed away from strong odors such as litter boxes and chemicals. It's not fair to them, and they can develop finicky eating habits.

Food and water should be kept in ceramic or stainless steel dishes, rather than in plastic ones. Some cats have an allergy to plastic, and ceramic and stainless steel are more sanitary. The food dishes should be flat-bottomed with low sides. Food bowls should be washed thoroughly after each meal.

Water

You should provide your cat with fresh water at all times. The water should be changed several times a day to prevent bacteria from building up in the dish.

If your cat eats canned food as a large part of her diet, she'll get water in her food and may drink less from her water dish. However, you must still leave fresh, clean water available for your cat at all times.

Some cats prefer to drink from a running-water source. My cat Taffy likes to drink from the kitchen faucet. This is fine, but it should not be the cat's only source of water.

Some cats prefer to drink directly from the tap.

Milk is not a necessary part of your cat's diet and may cause diarrhea. Feed your cat milk only if she can tolerate it, and then only allow small quantities. If your cat is milk intolerant but still enjoys it, try feeding plain yogurt as a treat.

Alcohol should *never* be offered to cats. It will not digest properly and can cause liver damage, even in small quantities.

Obesity

In today's health-conscious society, almost everyone is concerned about calories and losing weight. Yet we continue to over-indulge our felines until their sides bulge and they are tipping the scales.

> ## *Bathroom Safety*
>
> Cats sometimes like to drink from the toilet bowl, because the water is renewed often and is cold. While this is generally not recommended (cats can fall in and become trapped in the cold water), if you do let your cat drink from the bowl (or if she sneaks a sip while you're brushing your teeth), don't use toilet bowl cleaners that release chemicals with every flush. And make sure you rinse the bowl thoroughly every time you clean it.

Obesity is the most common nutritional disease in cats today. It is estimated that 12 percent of all housecats are overweight, with females having the highest incidence. This is no more healthy for your cat than it is for you. Obesity can cause heart trouble, respiratory difficulty, stress, low heat tolerance and a lowered resistance to illnesses. Obese cats can also have trouble bathing themselves and may allow their grooming habits to slide. Obese cats tend to die much younger than cats of proper weight. The average life span of an obese cat is six to 12 years old, compared with a 15- to 20-year life span for an indoor cat of ideal weight.

A cat that is approximately 15 to 25 percent over her ideal body weight is usually considered obese. To tell if your cat is overweight, place your hands on either side of her rib cage. If you cannot feel your cat's ribs through her fur, the animal is overweight (however, the ribs should *not* protrude).

Obesity is *not* caused by neutering a cat (as many have believed) or by keeping your cat indoors. Obesity in cats is caused by the same thing as it is in humans: eating more calories than are needed to sustain their activity level. Many people allow their cat to eat anything she wants. They get tired of the cat's incessant meowing and begging for food, so they give in. This can be a fatal mistake.

Although most cats are nibblers and only pick a little bit all day long, some will practically inhale their food as if it were their last meal. You must know your cat's eating habits in order to know how and when to feed. Some cats can have food in their dishes all day and will regulate themselves. Other must be fed a set amount at a specific time, or they will overeat.

Dieting Tips for Cats

+ Provide your cat with plenty of toys and scheduled playtimes.
+ Two or three small meals a day are preferable to one large meal.
+ Treats should be restricted to a small handful of dry food that would normally be a part of the cat's regular meal.
+ Try to avoid feeding your cat table scraps.
+ A high-fiber, low-fat, low-calorie food should be fed a cat that needs to shed weight. Food should be changed over gradually by mixing a little more diet food with the regular food each day until the cat is eating all diet food. The high-fiber food will make your cat feel full, allowing you to feed less.

If your cat is on a diet, don't expect immediate results. Cutting back on food intake will decrease your cat's metabolic rate, therefore causing her to burn less calories, so be patient.

An obese cat should be thoroughly examined by a veterinarian to rule out the possibility of thyroid disease. Follow the veterinarian's recommendations on diet and exercise.

Finicky Eaters

Does it seem that no matter what you try to feed your cat, she turns her nose up and walks away? Your cat is finicky. Many well-meaning owners allow their cats to become finicky eaters by removing a food the cat will not eat or only feeding one preferred food all the time. Before dubbing your cat finicky, check the following to be sure something else is not the cause:

+ Food dishes. Some cats won't eat out of deep dishes or dishes that are dirty. Use shallow dishes and keep them clean.
+ Have you recently changed foods? If your cat is not accustomed to a different food, try making the change gradually.

+ Is your cat on any medications? Some medicines may dull your cat's appetite or make certain foods taste different, causing the cat to avoid them.
+ Canned food that is cold from being in the refrigerator may not be palatable to some cats. Warm food to room temperature before feeding.

Then again, some cats are just plain finicky. With a finicky eater, leave food out for only 10 or 15 minutes at a time, then remove it whether or not the cat has eaten. This will give your cat the message, "Either you eat or you go hungry." However, do not let your cat go more than 24 hours without food.

Try mixing small amounts of a different food with your cat's favorite food, each day adding more and more of the other food. Do this with different flavors and varieties.

Do not allow food to go stale. Most cats like fresh food and may turn their noses up at food that has been sitting out.

Finicky eating is not harmful in itself, as long as the cat is eating a nutritionally complete cat food. However, you should try to prevent

Most times, finicky eaters are made, not born.

finicky behavior because someday your cat may need to go on a special diet, and a picky cat will probably turn her nose up at whatever you feed her. Also, your cat's favorite food may go off the market, leaving you with no choice but to choose another food. If your cat is lost, she probably will not be able to get her preferred food, as well.

Often stress will cause a cat to go off her food. If this seems to be the case, you will have to find the cause of the stress as soon as possible to get your cat eating again (see Chapter Three for more on stress).

The weather may affect your cat's food intake, as well. Although outdoor cats are more affected than indoor cats by changes in weather and seasons, an indoor cat, too, may show small differences in her eating habits due to seasonal changes.

Being finicky should not be confused with a nibbler or a cat refusing to eat due to illness. If your cat refuses to eat even her favorite foods after several days, it is time for a trip to the veterinarian. Any refusal to eat, even for a day, accompanied by vomiting, diarrhea, listlessness, panting or lethargy is the sign of a medical problem—go straight to the vet.

Treats and Table Scraps

Feeding treats and table scraps is acceptable, as long as you do not feed too much. The best treats to feed are snacks made especially for cats. There are many brands and flavors available for you to choose from.

Do not feed your cat raw meat, poultry or fish, as they can contain parasites, toxoplasmosis or salmonella. Cook any meats thoroughly and remove all bones before giving the meat to your cat. Never feed a cat anything with caffeine and never feed chocolate. Not only are these things unhealthy, they can be lethal to a cat.

Growing lawn grass especially for your cats is a good idea, especially for the indoor cat. Cats in the wild enjoy an occasional grass salad, and your indoor cat will, too. Growing grass for your cat has the added advantage that it will help keep her away from your houseplants.

Pet supply stores carry kits with seeds and a small container in which to grow the grass. You can also feed small amounts of lettuce and other vegetables if your cat will eat them, but not as a staple diet. Cats require greens to aid in digestion and pass hairballs, but they cannot digest them in large quantities.

Strange Eating Habits

Some cats develop the habit of sucking, chewing or even eating odd things, such as socks or blankets. It's not known exactly why some cats do this, and each cat's reason is most likely different. It may be a redirected suckling behavior—a leftover feeling of comfort from the days of suckling on mamma. Or maybe the cat needs something in her diet that she's not getting. The cause could also be stress or an eating disorder—something like a person who overindulges when he or she is depressed.

If your cat has this rather odd habit, as my cat Taffy does (she sucks and chews blankets, for her a form of suckling), don't worry. Usually this habit causes no difficulties. But be careful—watch that your cat does not ingest anything that contains hazardous chemicals. Also, stringy materials can cause blockages and problems within the intestinal tract.

If the problem gets out of hand, keep the preferred material out of your cat's reach and contact your veterinarian.

Vitamins and Minerals

As long as you feed your cat a diet that is complete for cats (as stated on the label), there will be no need to feed additional vitamins or minerals. Your cat will get enough of these in her diet, and extra supplements can be harmful.

There are certain situations, however, (such as metabolic difficulties, pregnant cats or young kittens) where a vitamin or mineral supplement may be needed. They should be given only under the advice of a veterinarian.

CHAPTER ELEVEN

Old Age

Is your cat beginning to gray around the whiskers? Or lazing around the house more and more, eating less and becoming crankier? She may be showing the signs of old age. At one time it was unusual for a cat to live past the age of 13 or 14. But now, with modern medicine, more people keeping their cats indoors, proper care and love, it is not uncommon to see a cat that is 18 or 20 years old.

Part of your responsibility when you acquire that cute little kitten is seeing her through her geriatric years. You lived with your cat, grew with your cat, shared happiness and tears with your cat. Now it's time to share in her old age and provide her with extra care during these sensitive years.

The old adage that one year of a cat's life is equivalent to seven years of a human's is a misconception. If that were true, a one-year-old cat would be the equivalent of a seven-year-old child. But a cat is psychologically and sexually mature at one year of age, while a seven-year-old child is not.

Rather, if you were to compare cat years with human years, you'd find cats age quicker than humans, and in stages. So a one-year-old cat is roughly equivalent to a human of approximately 18. A cat that is seven years old is reaching middle age. A 14-year-old cat is believed to be equal to a human in her 70s.

Although each cat ages at her own rate, just as humans do, an eight- to 10-year-old cat is considered at the beginning of her geriatric years.

The Geriatric Cat

As your cat ages, certain psychological and physiological changes will occur. Cats over the age of 10 years should have yearly geriatric screenings, along with their inoculations.

As their bodies change, older cats may develop problems with their bowels that can cause constipation, diarrhea or incontinence. If any problems should occur, take your cat to the veterinarian immediately.

Hearing and eyesight may begin to fail in an older cat, so steps should be taken to ensure the cat's safety. Cats may lose their eyesight due to glaucoma or cataracts. Cats usually adjust quite well to blindness. There are precautions you must take, however. Sharp objects should be removed and access to high places should be secured or blocked off. Do not move things around; a blind cat will become familiar with the placement of things and may become confused if things are placed differently. My blind cat, Teisha, gets around fine as long as everything is kept in its place, but the moment something is moved she becomes disoriented. Before touching or handling a blind cat, let your approach be known by speaking to the cat softly beforehand.

Older cats may lose their hearing, and you may notice a lack of normal responses because of this. Be sure to announce your approach to a hearing-impaired cat by touching the cat gently or letting the cat see you coming.

Signs of Old Age

As with humans, a cat's body goes through physiological changes as she ages: cloudy eyes, diminished hearing, graying fur, less luxuriant coat, flabby muscles, senility, stiffness, arthritis and decreased activity. As their metabolism slows, older cats become more susceptible to disease and are less able to regulate their body temperature. Therefore, it's important to keep your geriatric cat warm.

Older cats tend to have metabolism changes that may lead the cat to eat more or less than before. Often older cats, although their appetite may not change, will lose weight. This is normal, but it is important to

watch for signs of excessive weight
loss, which can indicate
a medical problem.
Your older cat may
become thin if she
does not get enough
protein in her diet.

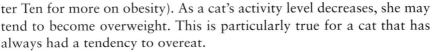

Obesity should also be
a concern for the owner
of a geriatric cat (see Chap-
ter Ten for more on obesity). As a cat's activity level decreases, she may
tend to become overweight. This is particularly true for a cat that has
always had a tendency to overeat.

An older cat's behavior may also change. Some cats become friendlier
with age, snuggling more and always in search of a warm lap to curl up
on. Others develop a grouchy attitude and become more easily agitated.

Litter box habits may also be affected by age. As a cat grows older,
watch for urinary problems. Inactivity, coupled with inability to hold
urine, may contribute to accidents. As your cat grows older, keep her
litter box near where the cat spends most of her time. You may even
wish to add another litter box so your cat will not have to go searching
for one, thus helping to avoid accidents.

A cat's coat quality and physical appearance may also deteriorate as
she ages. Some cats may neglect to groom themselves as often, so it is a
good idea to help by keeping up on your cat's grooming. This includes
care of the cat's nails. Not scratching regularly could cause an older cat's
nails to grow too long.

Care of the Aging Cat

Diet, exercise, grooming, nutrition, love, comfort and good medical care
are all major factors for you to consider as your cat gets on in years.

Food intake should be increased or decreased according to the cat's
weight (see Chapter Ten for more on diet). Allowing an older cat to
become too thin can be dangerous. If your older cat becomes sick, she
will need a little extra weight to get her through the illness.

But don't overdo it. Obesity can be a health hazard to any cat, but is
particularly so with an older cat. A cat that is carrying around too much
extra weight may live a shorter life than a cat whose weight is under

control. Weigh your cat regularly to ensure she is maintaining the proper weight. An older cat's weight may be slightly lower than a younger cat's, but should not be excessively so.

A good 100 percent nutritionally complete cat food especially made for geriatric cats is ideal for weight control. There are many good brands on the market today. Consult your veterinarian for his or her recommendation.

An older cat's sense of smell may diminish, causing the cat to have less interest in food. This could lead to the cat becoming underweight and undernourished, making her more susceptible to disease. A cat food with a stronger aroma may entice the cat to eat.

Keep your cat active with daily play, within the confines of your cat's physical abilities. Cats become less active as they grow older, and you will need to entice and encourage your cat with her favorite toys. If your cat is able and it is not too stressful for her, drag a string up and down the hallway or stairs or roll a ball along the floor so she can give chase. Catnip (for cats that will respond to it) is a good pick-me-up for an inactive cat.

An older cat will need much more love and TLC. The geriatric cat may choose to curl up with you on your lap and spend more time being near you. Never be stingy with your attention, as an older cat may appreciate and need it more. If your cat becomes grouchier as she ages, patience on your part is a must.

A slower approach may be necessary with an aging cat. As their senses go, cats become a little less secure emotionally. They need you to understand their slower behavior and give them extra love and attention.

Gum disease is very common with older cats and may affect your older cat's eating habits. Regular dental care is important. Have your cat's teeth checked once or twice a year. You may wish to help by brushing your cat's teeth yourself, if she will allow you to (this is easier if you accustomed your cat to having her mouth touched and opened at a young age). Using a strip of gauze wrapped around your finger, you can rub your cat's teeth with a special cat toothpaste. Don't use human toothpaste, as it causes excessive salivation and can create an upset stomach if swallowed.

The comfort of the aging cat is an important consideration. Older cats may require more warmth than before, so take extra precautions to keep the cat warm. On chilly days or nights, keep windows closed so the cat does not get near a draft.

What If Something Happens to You?

You know your cat needs extra care as she ages. But what about providing for your cat(s) in the event something happens to you? This is something you must think about, because often animals that are not specifically mentioned in a will end up in pounds or shelters where they are either adopted out (possibly to someone who will not care for them as you did) or put down.

While you cannot leave money to your cats, you can leave your cats in a specific person's care. If you know of someone who would be able to care for your cats, then name her or him (with their permission, of course) in your Will as the cats' caretaker. You should also designate a sum of money to go to that person to care for the cats.

If there is no one you know who can care for your cats in a manner you see fit (including making sure they remain indoors), then you may want to find a no-kill cat shelter where your cats will either be adopted (usually no-kill shelters have stricter screening rules) or live their lives in the shelter. Investigate to find a shelter that is clean, to your liking and has a good reputation.

Make sure you state specifically in your Will that your cats are to remain indoor cats and, if you choose to bequeath your cats to a no-kill shelter, it's nice to leave a healthy donation for their benefit.

Health Problems

Regular veterinary exams are a must as your cat gets older. Kidney disease can plague older cats, so watch the cat's normal intake of water and her urinary habits. If your cat seems to be drinking an excessive amount of water, urinating often or straining, it's time for a trip to the veterinarian. Your cat should also have a checkup if she has any change in litter box habits.

Hyperthyroidism is also common in older cats. If your cat seems to consume more food than normal, urinates more often and drinks more water, take her to the veterinarian to be checked for an enlarged thyroid gland.

Diabetes is also common in older cats. Some symptoms include increased appetite with weight loss, drinking excessive amounts of water and urinating more frequently.

If you suspect any of these problems, do not hesitate to contact your veterinarian. You will need to keep a close eye on your older cat's health and habits. Keep up with your home health exams (as described in Chapter Eight) and perform them more frequently. Pay special attention to your cat's teeth. Excessive tartar buildup can lead to gum disease and tooth loss. Also, pay close attention when massaging your cat's body. All lumps should be checked by your veterinarian to be sure they are not cancerous.

Once per year, your older cat should have a geriatric screening done by your veterinarian. This includes a blood count, urinalysis, fecal exams and blood profiles. This will alert you early to any problems so they can be treated before they become too widespread. Cancers of the blood, lymphatic system and gastrointestinal tract, as well as thyroid problems, are more prevalent with older cats, and regular blood tests can help uncover these problems at early stages.

Loss and Grieving

There comes an unhappy time in all cat owners' lives when they must say goodbye to a cherished feline. Often you are faced with the difficult choice of euthanasia when a cat is seriously ill. It would be selfish to allow a cat to go on living if the animal is in pain and there is nothing more that can be done. This is never an easy decision to make, and it may be difficult to know when the right time is to make it. Talk to your veterinarian, and ask as many questions as you need to in order to thoroughly understand your cat's situation.

If you do make this decision, stay with your cat until the end. It will be hard, but remember: Your cat was a loyal companion to you, and she deserves to have the familiarity of your presence in her last moments.

Letting go is an important step in coping with the loss of a beloved cat. It is normal to feel all the usual signs of depression when a cat dies. Don't be afraid to hurt, and don't let anyone try to minimize your grief.

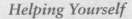

Helping Yourself

- ✦ Acknowledge the inevitability of your cat's death.
- ✦ Hold a ceremony to finalize the act and pay tribute to your cat.
- ✦ Allow yourself to mourn freely.
- ✦ Seek out family and friends who understand. Don't be afraid to talk about it.
- ✦ Don't fear your emotions.
- ✦ Plant a tree or flower in honor of your pet.

Denial is a natural first stage that most people go through. It is difficult to accept the loss of someone so loved. The next stage of grief is generally anger and/or guilt. These are normal, but you should not focus on them. Instead, think of the good times you had with kitty. Do not dwell on your depression.

Plan a burial or a memorial ceremony. There are pet cemeteries around the country, and you may want to consider a service at one near you. Here you can visit kitty whenever you wish and even bring her favorite flowers.

If you find the grief too much to handle, there are support groups where pet owners get together to discuss their losses. It can help to speak to others who have experienced the same pain.

If you have other pets, do not deny them your love and attention. They will feel the loss as well, so play with them and let them know you still love and care for them, too.

(Craig Zeichner)

Give yourself time to recover. Do not let your loss deter you from acquiring another companion. You will never be able to replace your cat, but there are many wonderful cats out there just waiting to share with you all the love and attention you have to give.

Remember that you gave your cat the best possible home you could and that your pet is in a pleasant place, romping, playing and happy.

INDEX

Common ailments,
138–40
Companion for cat,
61
Communication, 62
Competition, 49–50
Confinement stress,
41
Convulsion/seizure,
156
Corncob litter, 72–73
Cornish Rex, 122
Coughing, 138
Crate training, 37–38
Creeping Charlie, 16
Creeping fig, 16

D

Daffodil, 16
Deaf cats, 42
Death and divorce, 56
Declawing, 83–84,
106–8
Diapers, 88
Diarrhea, 139
Dieffenbachia, 16
Dieting tips, 176
Dishes
food, 14
water, 14
Dogs
dangers, 5
introduction, 31–32
Dry food, 172

E

Ear drops, 149
Ear mites. *See* Mites
Earthquakes. *See*
Natural disasters

Eating habits
changes in, 58
finicky, 176–78
strange, 179
Electrical cords, 18–19
Electrical shock,
153–54
Emergencies
approach, 150–51
first-aid kit, 151
household, 149–50
natural, 158–61
preparation, 150
Emotional changes, 47
English ivy, 16
Environmental
changes, 47
Environmental issues,
10
Exercise, 61
Eye ointment and
drops, 149
Eyes, object in, 156

F

Fear, 60
Feeding, 173
finicky cats,
176–78
milk, 174
obesity, 174–76
stale food, 177
strange eating
habits, 179
treats, 178
vegetables, 171
vitamins and
minerals, 179
water, 174
Feline Immunodefi-
ciency Virus (FIV), 5

Feline Infectious
Peritonitis (FIP), 5
Feline Leukemia Virus
(FeLV), 5
Feline rivalry, 47–48
Feline T-Lymphocytic
Virus (FTLV), 5
Finicky eating, 176–78
Fireplaces, 18
First aid, 151
Fleas, 5, 142
Flexor tendonectomy,
109
Frontline flea preven-
tative, 143

G

Games, 62-64
Getting lost, 6. *See
also* Lost cat
Geriatric cat, 182
Good nutrition, 60
Grain litter, 73–74
Grass litter, 73
Grooming, 112–17
dematting,
116–17
longhaired cat,
114–16
shorthaired cat,
117–18
Grooming tools, 114

H

Hair balls, 139
Handicapped cats, 42,
66
Harnesses, 130
Health, 133–61
exam, 134–36